Piano Technique

Book 5

Authors
Barbara Kreader, Fred Kern, Phillip Keveren, Mona Rejino

Director, Educational Keyboard Publications
Margaret Otwell

Editor
Carol Klose

Illustrator
Fred Bell

Book: ISBN 978-0-634-01357-7
Book/CD: ISBN 978-0-634-08979-4

Dear Teacher,

Piano Technique Book 5 presents a *Warm-Up* and an *Etude* for each new technical skill students will encounter in **Piano Lessons Book 5**.

We suggest that you demonstrate each *Warm-Up*. Teaching by demonstration allows students to focus on the purely physical aspects of learning a new skill, such as hand and body position, or arm and finger movement. This helps them understand the connection between the movement they make and the sound they create.

Once students have learned the physical skill presented in each *Warm-Up*, they can use it to play the corresponding *Etude* with expression.

The *Musical Fitness Plan* on each warm-up page teaches new technical concepts and provides a checklist for technical readiness:

- **Playing Broken Chords in One Phrase between Hands**
- **Playing *Tenuto* in One Hand and *Staccato* in the Other**
- **Coordinating Right-Hand and Left-Hand Phrases of Different Lengths**
- **Playing Broken Chords That Use Finger Substitution**
- **Contracting the Hand to Accommodate a New Position**
- **Moving from Hand to Hand Within a Phrase**
- **Playing *Legato* Parallel Fifths**
- **Accommodating Different Black Keys When Moving from One Scale to Another**
- **Playing Grace Notes**
- **Playing Blocked Chords in First Inversion**
- **Playing Blocked Chords in Second Inversion**
- **Keeping the Hand in Position When Playing Parallel Chords**
- **Playing a Waltz Bass**
- **Playing a Chromatic Scale**
- **Playing Blocked Chords *Legato***
- **Combining Patterns of First and Second Inversion Chords**

By the end of **Piano Technique Book 5**, students will be able to play the C, G, F, D, and B♭ Major scales, and the A, E, D, B, and G Minor scales. They will also be able to play the I, IV, V7, I chord progression in those keys in root, close, and open positions, both blocked and broken. Having learned all these skills, students will have the confidence to move on to intermediate piano literature.

Best wishes,

Barbara Kreader Fred Kern
Phillip Keveren Mona Rejino

Dear Students,

You need an exercise plan to stay physically fit.

Like participating in sports, playing the piano is a physical activity that uses your whole body. **Piano Technique Book 5** will outline the *Musical Fitness Plan* you need to develop new musical skills.

Your *Musical Fitness Plan* includes:

- **Warm-Ups** – drills to develop new musical skills
- **Etudes** – music to practice using the new skills you learned in the *Warm-Ups*

It feels good to play the piano! Your teacher will show you how to play each *Warm-Up*. Follow the *Musical Fitness Plan*, paying careful attention to the way you use your body, arms, and fingers to create music. When you play, notice how the movement you make affects the sound you create. Once you have learned each *Warm-Up*, read and practice the matching *Etude*.

You are now ready to begin.

Have fun!

Barbara Kreader Fred Kern
Phillip Keveren Mona Rejino

Piano Technique Book 5

CONTENTS

** Students can check activities as they complete them.*

Musical Fitness Review

Use the following checklist to demonstrate the skills you learned in **Book 4**.

- ☐ **Crossing 2 over 1**
- ☐ **Playing One Hand *Legato* and the Other *Staccato***
- ☐ **Syncopation Between Hands**
- ☐ **Syncopated Pedaling**
- ☐ **Tucking 1 under 3; Crossing 3 over 1**
- ☐ **Crossing One Hand over Another**
- ☐ **Combining Musical Fitness Skills**
  - Playing in Extended Positions
  - Changing Positions
  - Playing Chords
  - Playing Black-key/White-key Combinations
- ☐ **Playing Blocked and Broken Chords in Close Position**
- ☐ **Playing a Left-hand Melody and Right-hand Accompaniment**
- ☐ **Sustaining One Note while Playing Another Note in the Same Hand**
- ☐ **Substituting One Finger for Another**
- ☐ **Extending to an Octave**

Full Circle
Review Etude

Using all the confidence you gained in **Piano Technique Book 4**, celebrate your new musical skills! Play each phrase with a downward motion of the arm, ending with an upward motion of the wrist.

Musical Fitness Plan

Use this checklist to review fitness skills and to focus on learning new ones.

☐ **Changing Positions**

☐ **Syncopated Pedaling**

☐ **Extending to an Octave**

☐ **Playing Black-key/White-key Combinations**

Playing *Legato* Broken Chords Between the Hands

Strive for a smooth follow-through from one hand to the other. Release the broken chord with an upward motion of the wrist as the other hand enters with a downward motion of the arm.

Playing *Tenuto* in One Hand and *Staccato* in the Other

Play the *staccato* notes in one hand with a gently bouncing wrist, letting go of each note as soon as you play it. In the other hand, play the *tenuto* notes with a downward motion of your arm, using a weighted, detached touch.

***To the Teacher:** Demonstrate these warm-ups first. This will allow students to focus on the purely physical aspects of learning a new skill. Encourage students to play each warm-up in different octaves.*

Warm-Ups

Waterfall *pg. 8*

When water cascades over rocks, it falls in one fluid motion.

Follow through smoothly from one hand to the other. Release the broken chord with an upward motion of your wrist as your other hand enters with a downward motion of your arm.

Build the dynamics from *pianissimo* to *mezzo forte* and back to *pianissimo* by varying the arm weight you use on each downward motion.

Elves vs. Giants *pg. 9*

Create the sound of a contest between elves and giants by emphasizing the differences between the piano *and* forte *sections of this piece.*

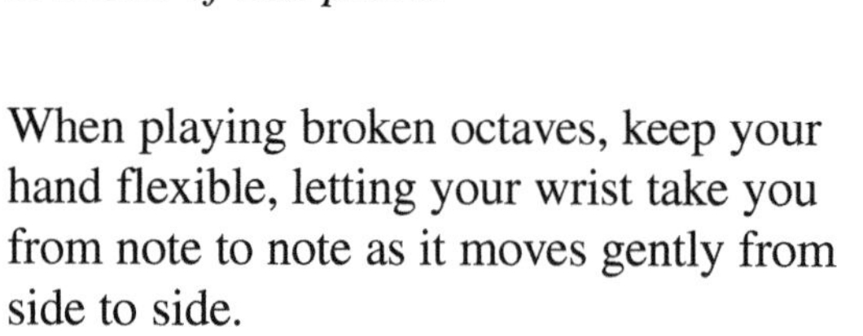

When playing broken octaves, keep your hand flexible, letting your wrist take you from note to note as it moves gently from side to side.

When playing a melodic pattern that uses sharps or flats, move your hand slightly forward into the black keys.

To create a strong *tenuto* sound, play with a weighted, detached touch, keeping the weight of your arm directly behind each finger. Listen for a slight break in sound between each note.

Waterfall

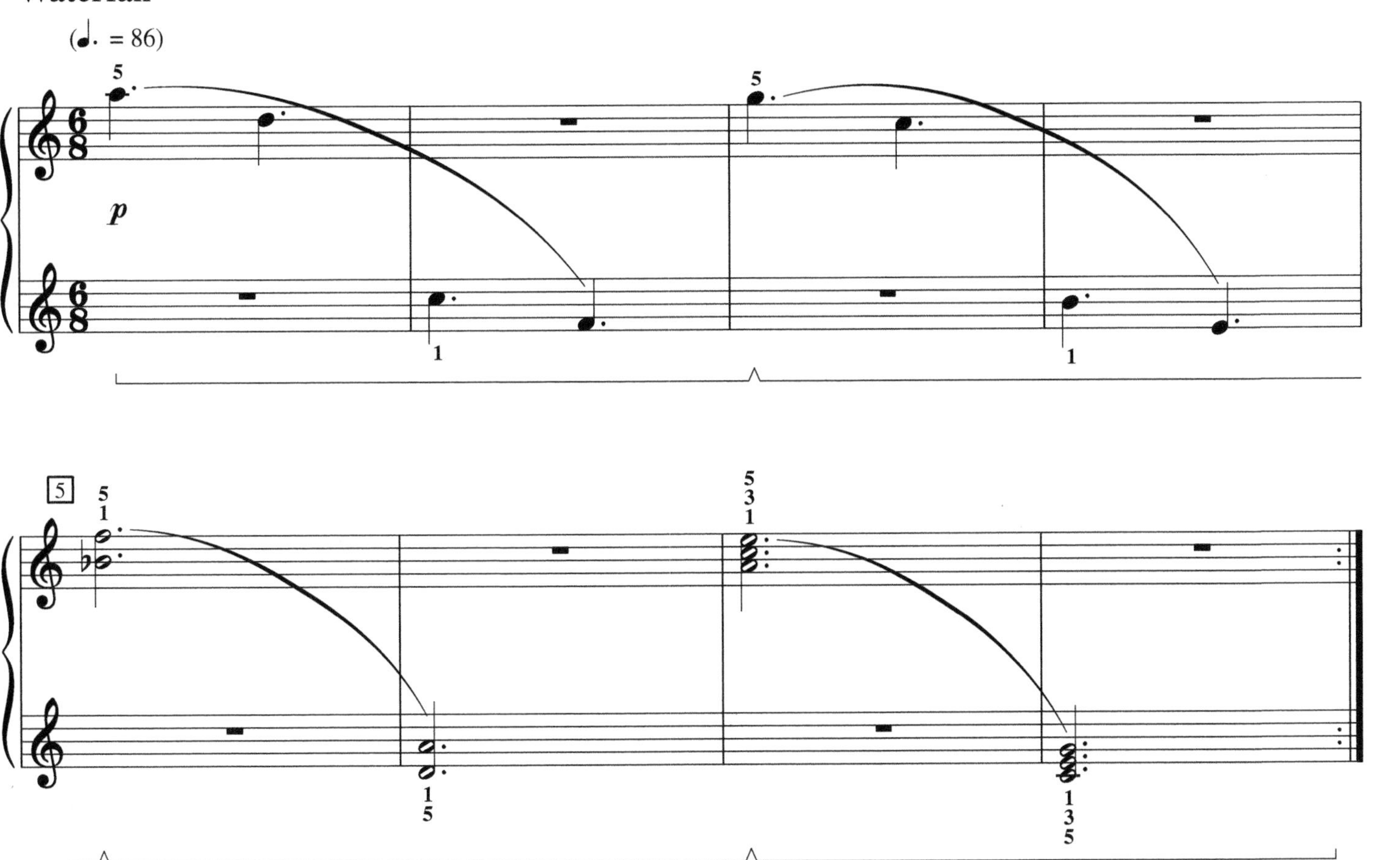

Elves vs. Giants

(♩ = 80)

Waterfall

Fluidly (♩. = 86) 5/6 4

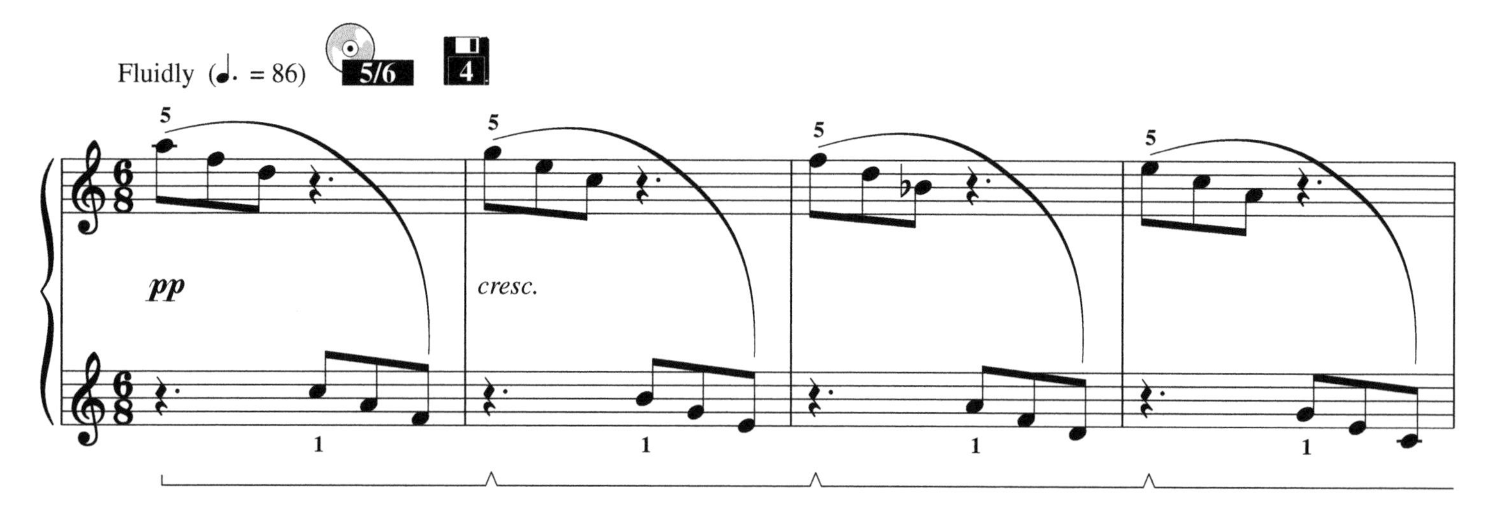

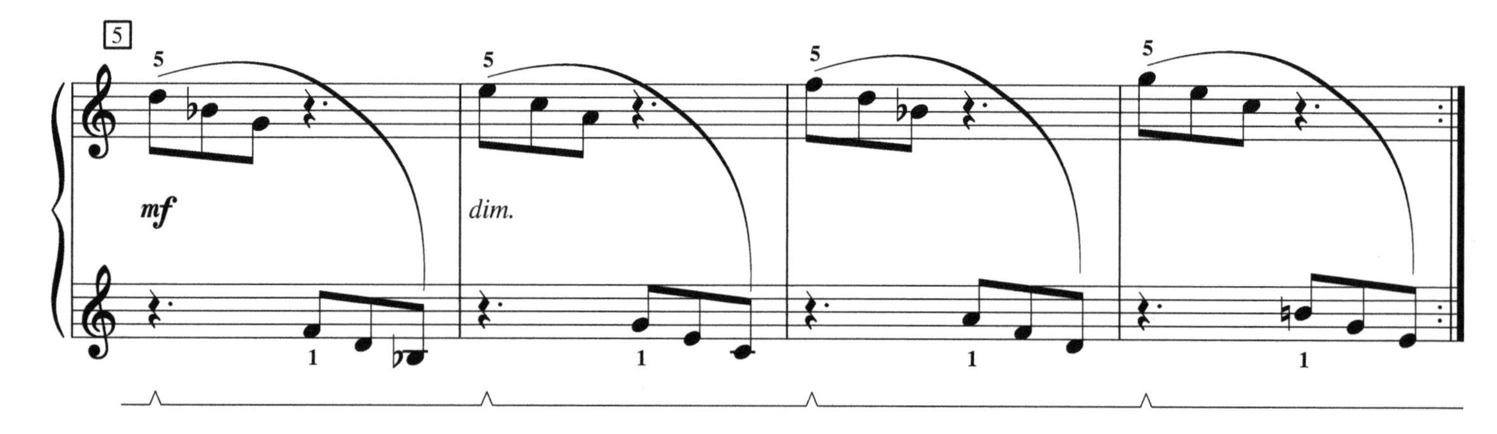

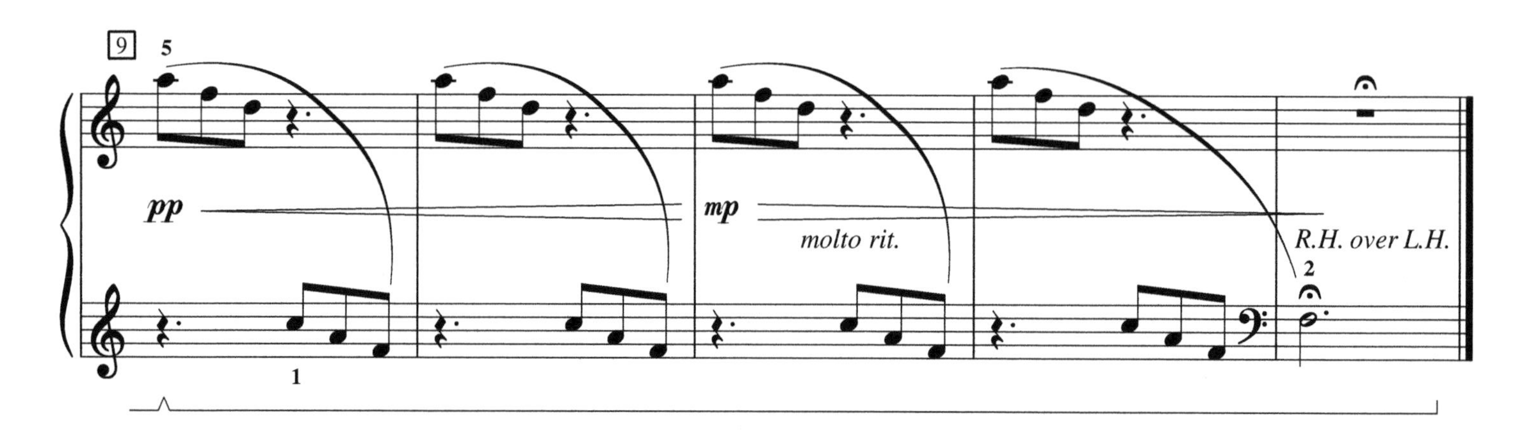

Elves vs. Giants

Use with Lesson Book 5, pg. 5

Musical Fitness Plan

Use this checklist to review fitness skills and to focus on learning new ones.

☐ **Crossing 2 over 1, and 3 over 1**

Coordinating Overlapping Right-hand and Left-hand Phrases

When you begin and release phrases at different times, play the last note of each phrase with an upward motion of the wrist. Listen for the slight break in sound between each phrase.

To the Teacher: *Continue to demonstrate these warm-ups first. Encourage students to create variations by moving the warm-ups to different octaves or transposing them to different keys.*

Warm-Ups

Instant Replay *pg. 12*

Televised sporting events often show an instant replay of a certain move or play. By watching their technique in these slow-motion video clips, athletes can better identify the particular movements that made the play a success.

Athletes can then repeat a skill over and over until their bodies can perform it automatically.

Observe your physical motions as you play **Instant Replay**. When crossing your second or third finger over your thumb, let your wrist and forearm follow through. Release your thumb the moment you play the next finger, moving your arm, hand, and fingers into position to play the next notes.

In the etude, play each left-hand five-finger pattern with a single drop/lift motion of your arm and wrist. Release the eighth-note as soon as you play it. When necessary, move to a new position during the eighth-note rest.

Step And Turn *pg. 13*

When two ballet dancers sweep across the stage together, the male dancer stops and supports the ballerina while she turns. Even though they begin and release their steps at different times, they work in close harmony with each other to create one unified movement.

In the etude, one hand "steps" while the other "turns." The hands begin and release their phrases at different times. Drop into the first note of each phrase or slur with a downward motion of your arm, and play the last note using an upward motion of your wrist. Listen for the slight break in sound between each phrase.

Instant Replay

Step And Turn

Instant Replay

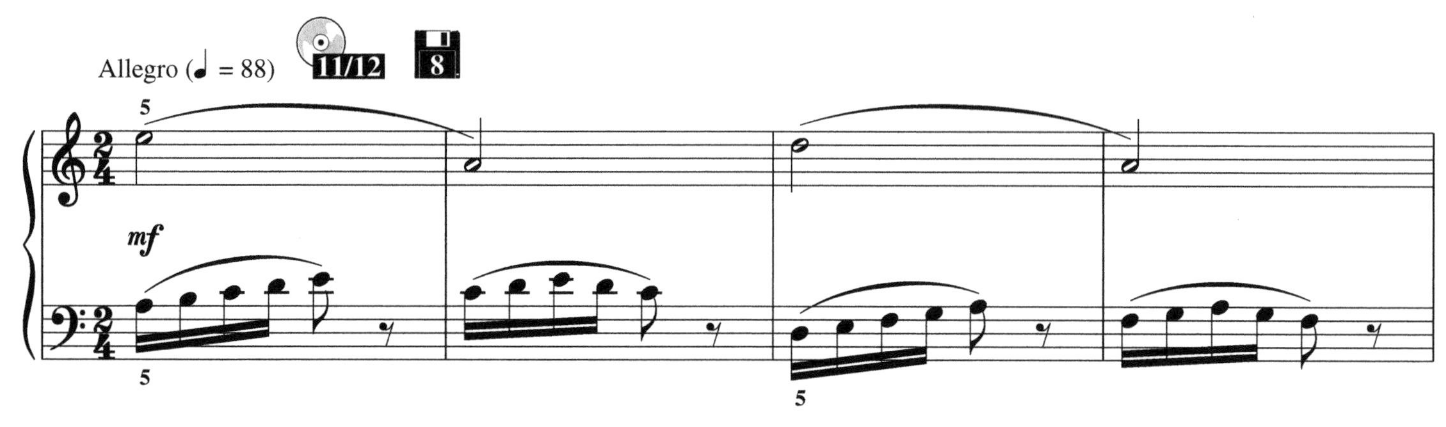

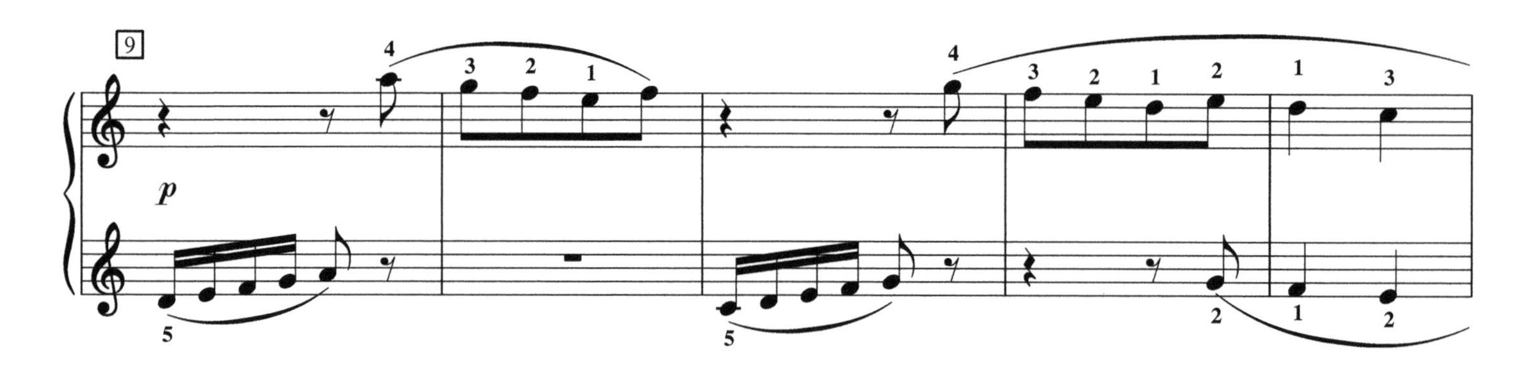

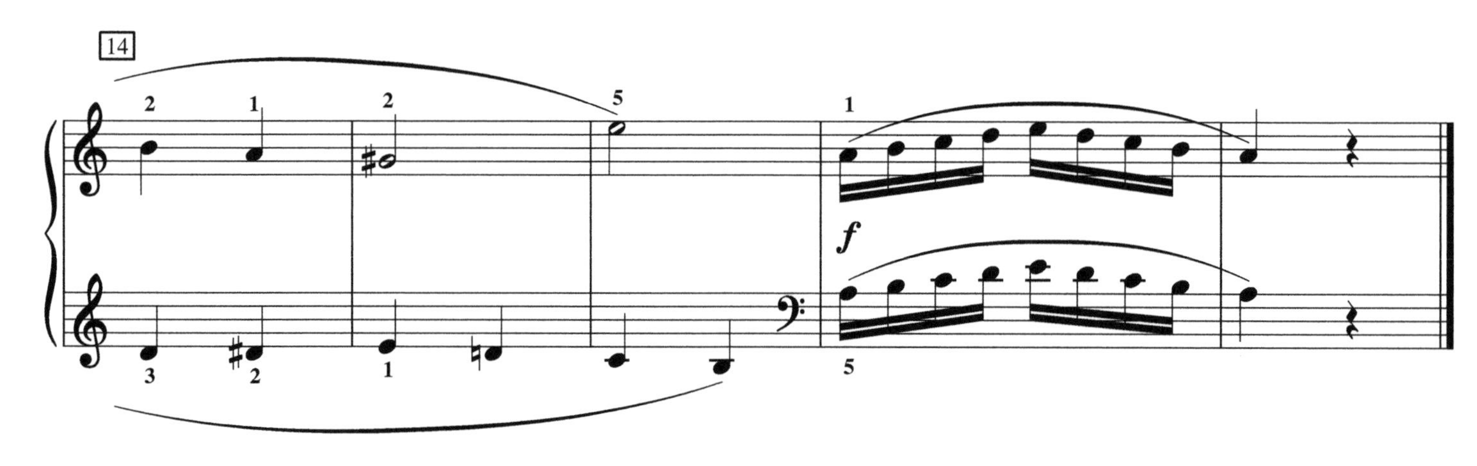

Step And Turn

Use with Lesson Book 5, pg. 11

Musical Fitness Plan

Use this checklist to review fitness skills and to focus on learning new ones.

☐ **Syncopation Between Hands**

Using Finger Substitutions

When you exchange one finger for another on a repeated note, release the first note with an upward motion of your wrist. Let your arm follow through to the new position. Play the repeated note using a downward motion of your arm.

To the Teacher: *Continue to demonstrate these warm-ups first. Encourage students to create variations by moving the warm-ups to different octaves.*

Warm-Ups

Rock Bottom *pg. 16*

Rock music pulsates with a steady, repeated bass. The bass guitarist and keyboard player join with the drummer to create the strong heartbeat of this music. The singers and the other musicians then add the melody, which often contains syncopated rhythm patterns that are repeated.

Keep the repeated notes pulsating by playing each one with a gently bouncing wrist.

To solve the technical difficulties of playing the syncopated rhythms, first tap and count them away from the keyboard.

Tap and count:

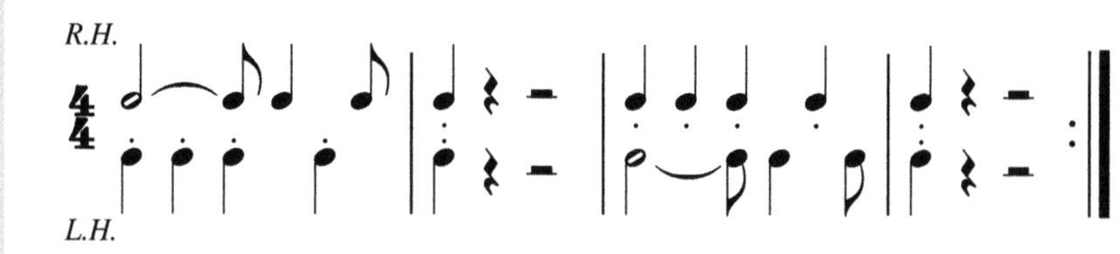

Alpine Echoes *pg. 17*

Imagine two alphorns echoing each other as they send resonant sounds into the mountain air. The moment one horn ends its melody, the other horn answers it, creating a musical dialogue between the instruments.

Imitate the musical conversation between the two alphorns by varying your arm weight to create different dynamics.

When substituting one finger for another on repeated notes, release the first note with an upward motion of your wrist. Let your arm follow through to the new position. Play the repeated note with the new finger, using a downward motion of your arm.

Rock Bottom

Alpine Echoes

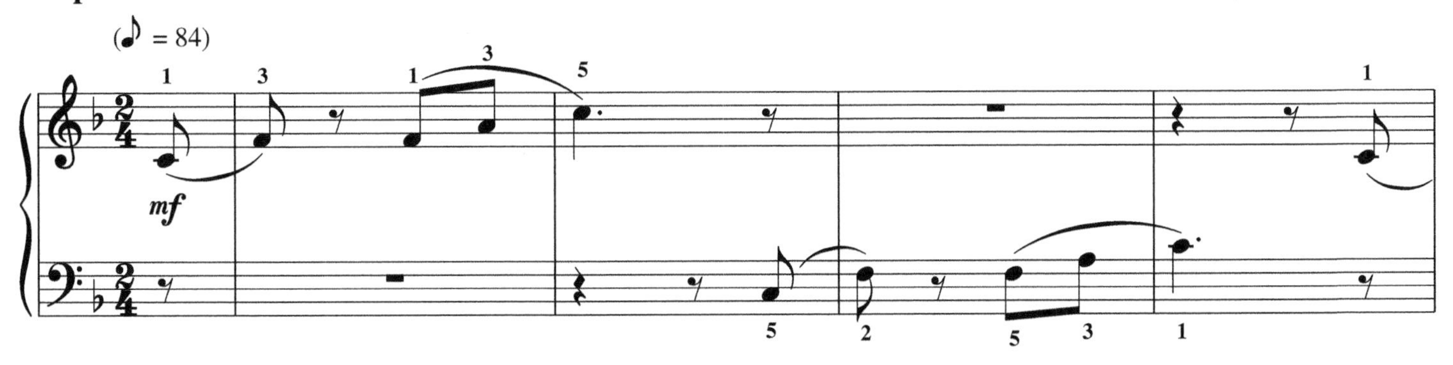

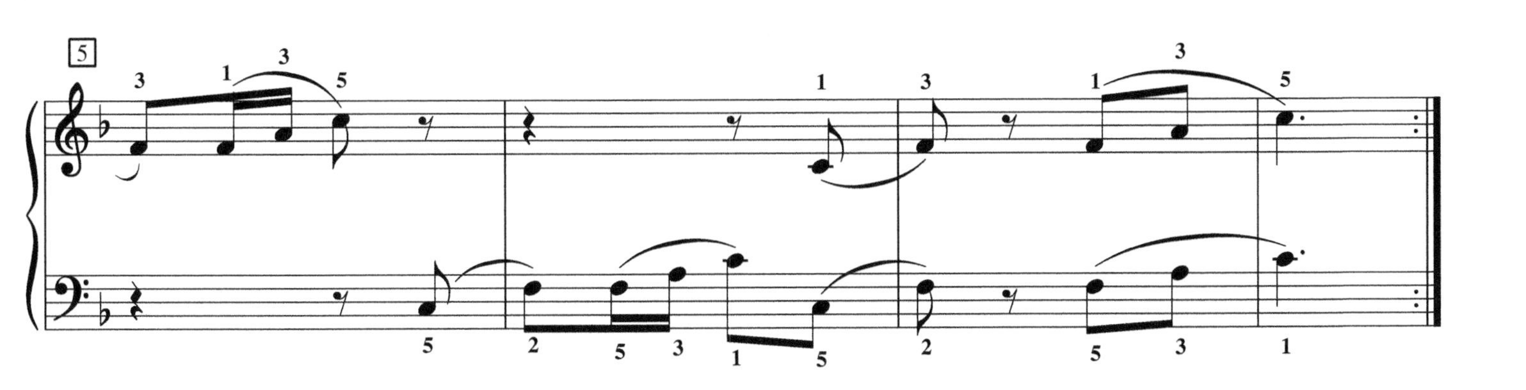

Rock Bottom

Alpine Echoes

Musical Fitness Plan

Use this checklist to review fitness skills and to focus on learning new ones.

☐ **Using Finger Substitutions**

Contracting the Hand to Accommodate a New Position
When moving from fingers 1 to 4, or 4 to 1, between phrases, close the hand slightly to accommodate the new position.

Moving from Hand to Hand within a Phrase
Create a seamless sound as you move hand to hand within a phrase by playing without any break in sound or gap in the rhythm.

To the Teacher: *Continue to demonstrate these warm-ups first. Encourage students to create variations of the warm-ups by moving them to different octaves.*

Warm-Ups

Bubble Trail *pg. 20*

When you release bubbles from a bubble wand, you stretch out your arm and slowly turn your body round and round in one continuous motion.

Play each phrase in one drop/lift motion, keeping your wrist flexible as you gently move from side to side. Match the tone of the last note of one phrase to the starting tone of the next.

In the etude, continue to create a seamless sound when moving from hand to hand within a phrase by playing without any break in sound or gap in rhythm.

Gyroscope *pg. 21*

A gyroscope is a wheel mounted in a ring so that its axis is free to move in any direction. As the wheel continues to spin, the ring smoothly rotates and changes direction.

Musical patterns that move in sequences are often easier to play if you use the same fingering for each one. Let the finger that begins each sequence lead the way, moving to the new position during the slight break in sound between phrases.

Bubble Trail

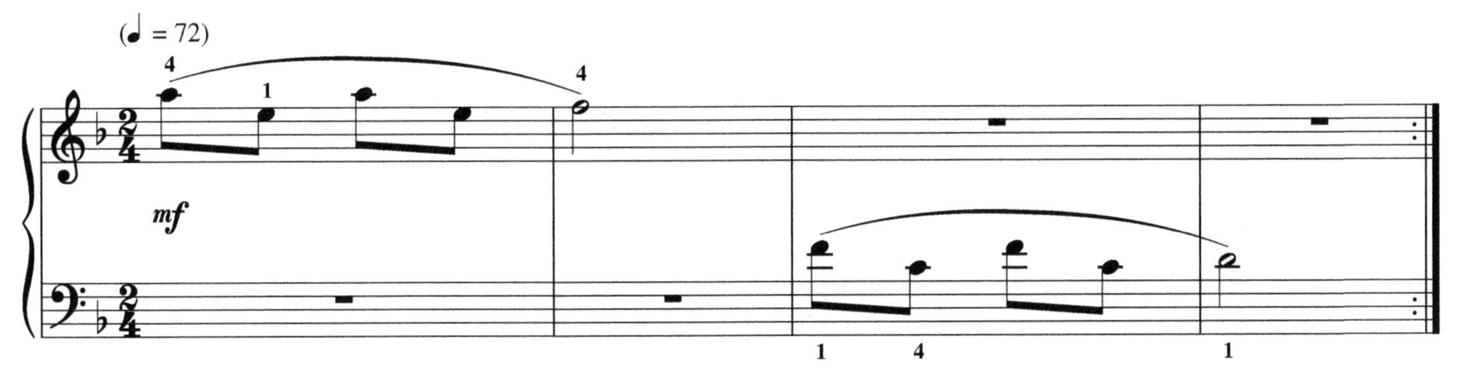

Gyroscope

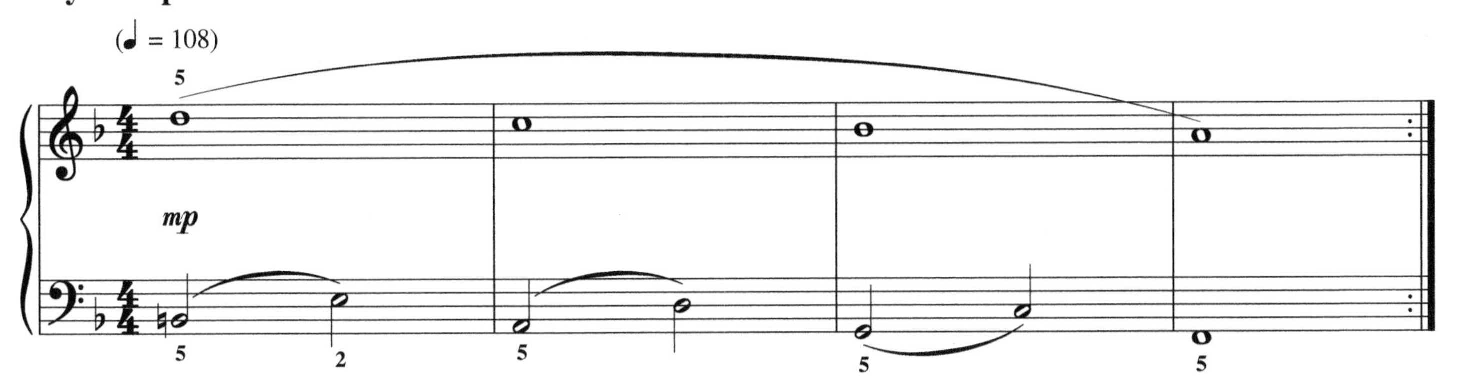

Bubble Trail

Gyroscope

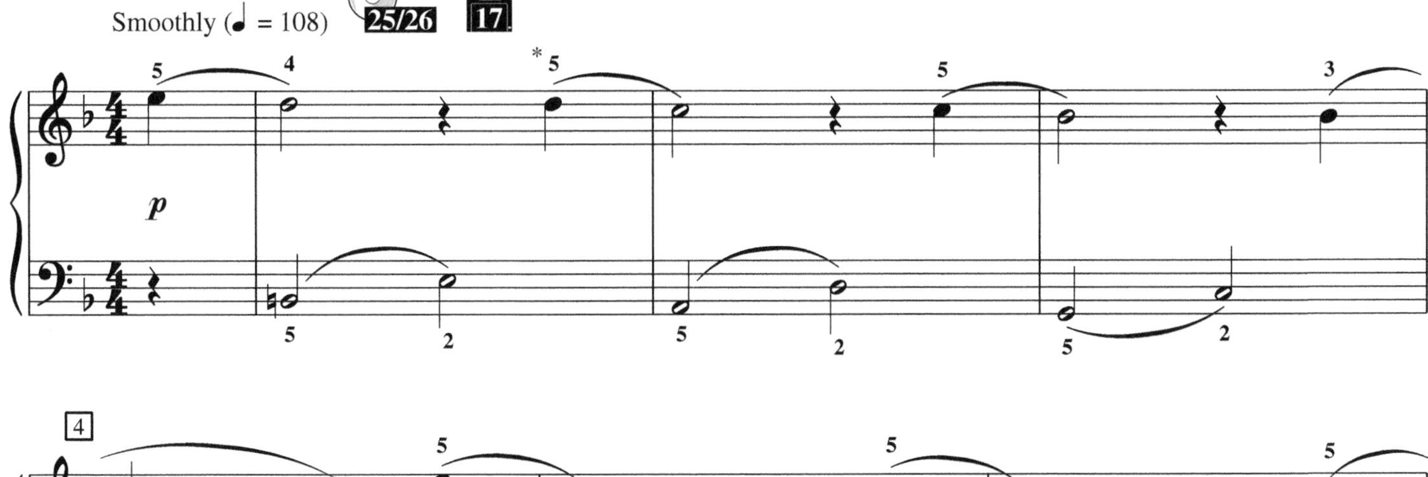

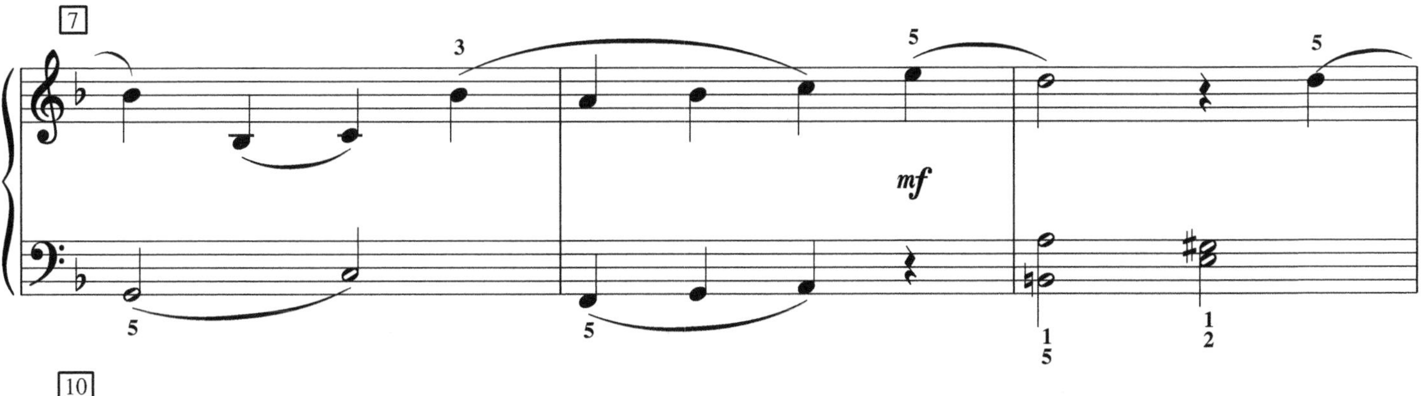

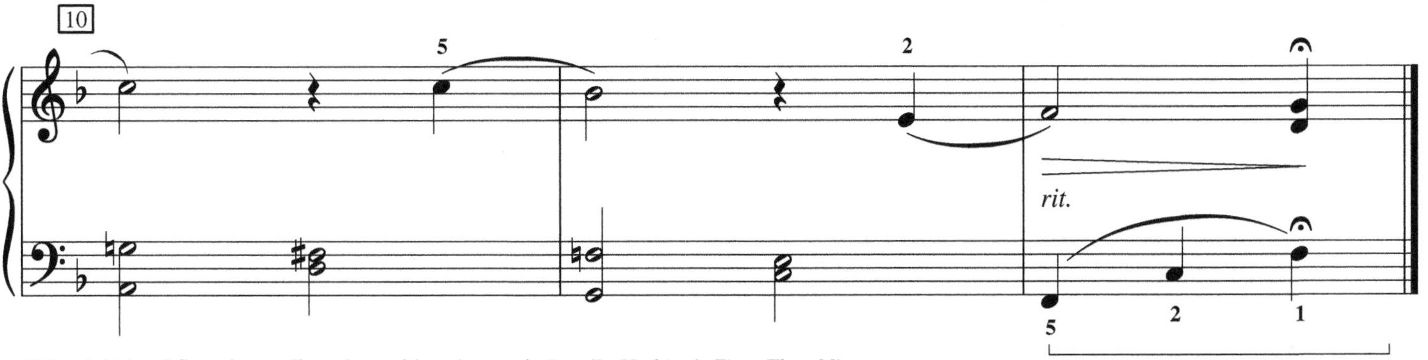

* The right-hand fingering outlines the position changes in Boyd's *Nothing's Finer Than Minor.*

Musical Fitness Plan

Use this checklist to review fitness skills and to focus on learning new ones.

☐ **Syncopated Pedaling**

☐ **Tucking 1 under 3; Crossing 3 over 1**

Playing *Legato* Parallel Fifths
Keep your hand in the basic shape of the interval. Use your arm to move as smoothly as possible from interval to interval, lightly touching the surface of the keys with your fingertips.

Accommodating Different Black Keys When Moving from One Scale to Another
Identify the name of the scales in the piece. Silently finger each scale on the keyboard several times, noticing the black-key/white-key combination for each one.

To the Teacher: *Continue to demonstrate these warm-ups first. Encourage students to create variations of the warm-ups by moving them to different octaves.*

Warm-Ups

Wide Open Spaces *pg. 24*

Widening the distance between chord tones by playing the third of the chord as a melody note in the right hand creates a warm, open sound. Composer Aaron Copland (1900-1999) often used this open arrangement of chord tones to evoke the mood created by the sight of the vast American landscape.

To create the sound of *legato* parallel fifths, keep your hand in the basic shape of the interval. Use your arm to move as smoothly as possible from fifth to fifth, keeping your fingers on the surface of the keys.

Although you will still hear a slight break in sound between the fifths, the smooth *legato* melody in the right hand will create the illusion that both hands are playing *legato*.

Evening Sky *pg. 25*

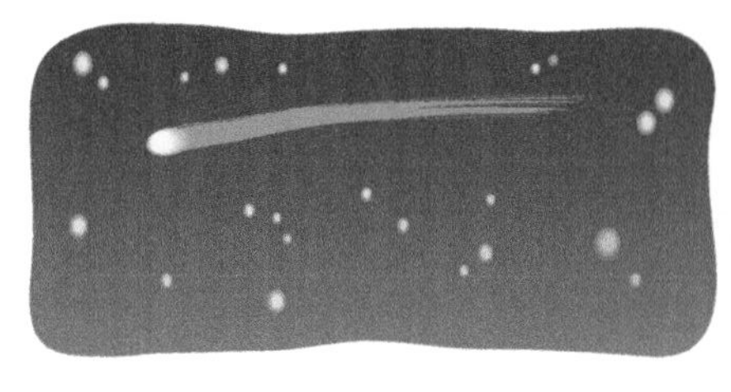

When we look up at the night sky, we expect to find each star hanging in its usual place. When a shooting star streaks through the dark, the predictable, sparkling picture quickly changes.

To create a sound-picture of the evening sky, play the left-hand phrases using little arm weight. Listen for a floating, effortless wash of sound.

When you play the scale passages, follow through with your arm in one sweeping motion. Gently release the last note of each right-hand phrase, using the slight break in sound to move to the next position.

Wide Open Spaces

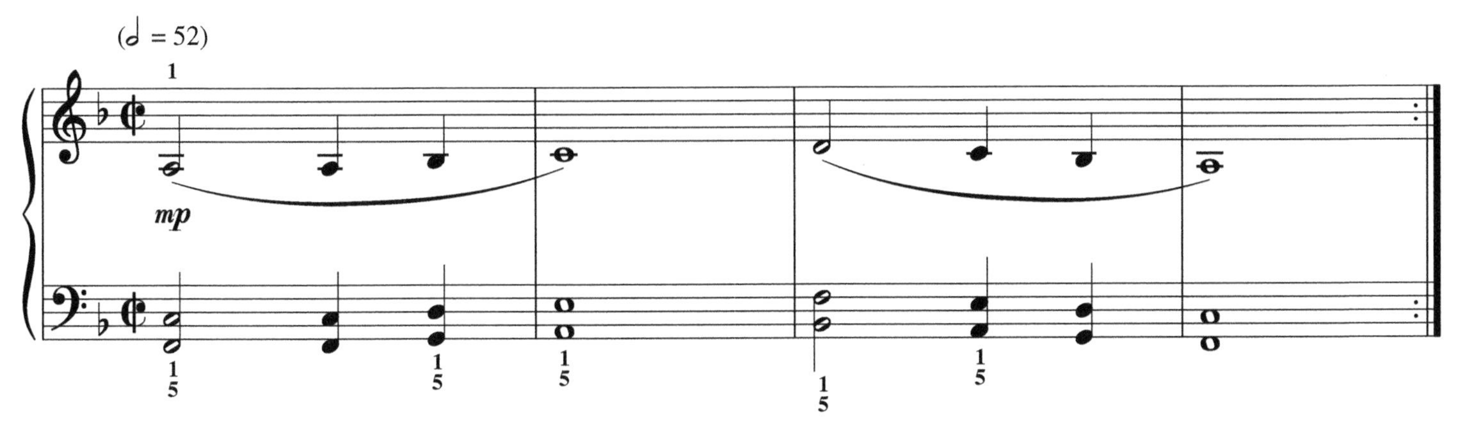

Evening Sky

Wide Open Spaces

Evening Sky

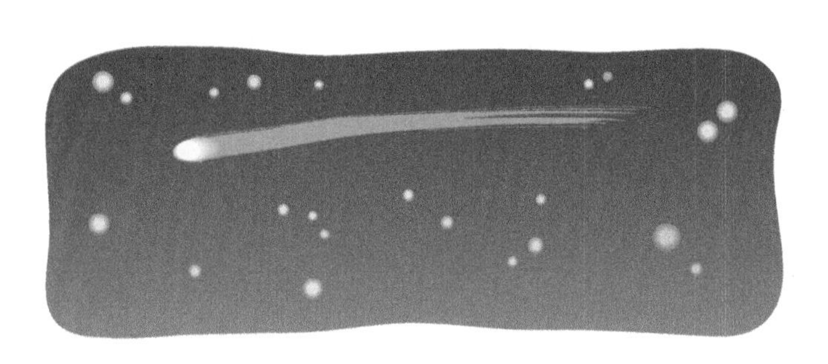

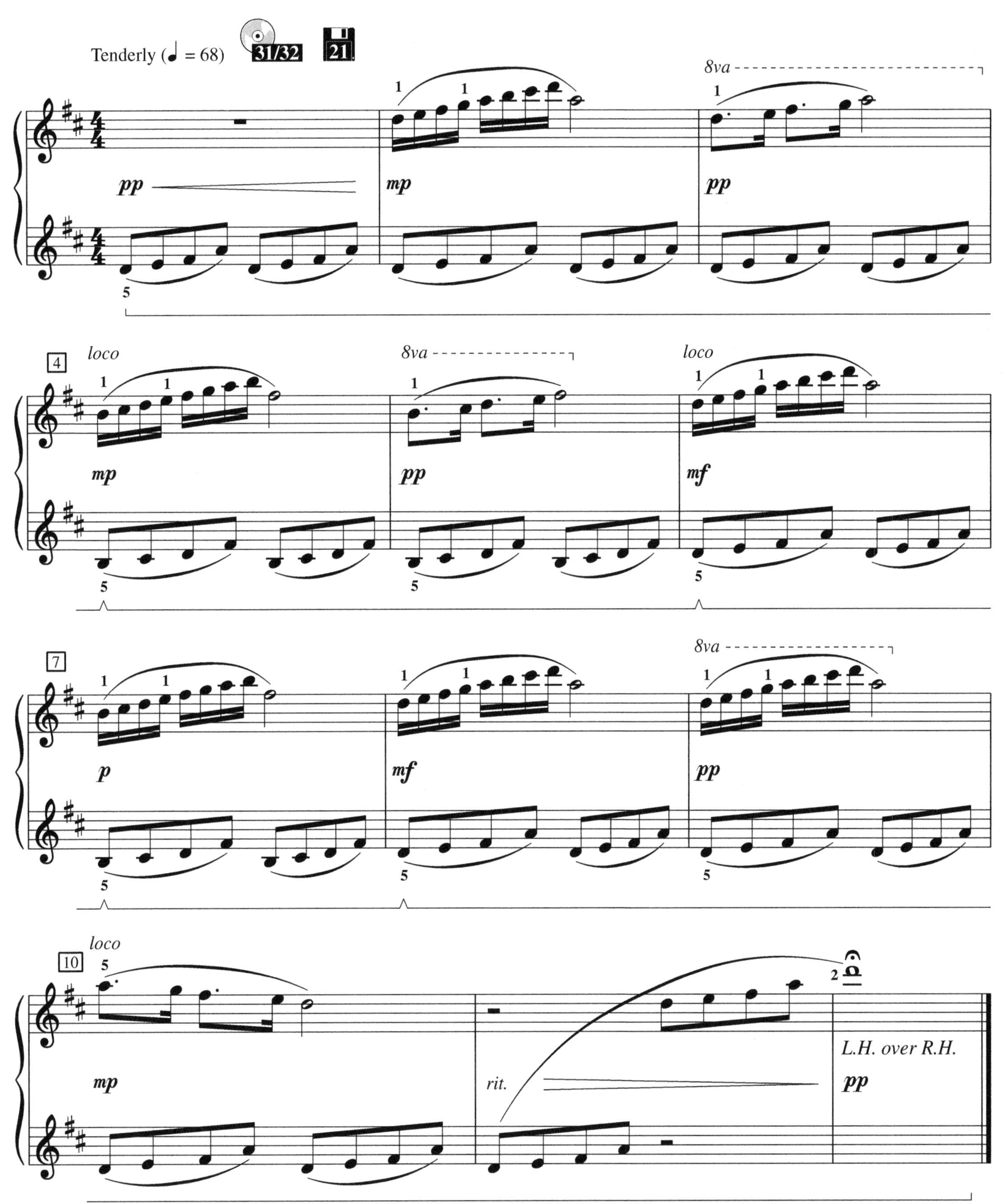

Musical Fitness Plan

Use this checklist to review fitness skills and to focus on learning new ones.

Playing Grace Notes

To play grace notes, use the same drop/lift motion of the arm and wrist used when playing two-note slurs, but compress the motion into one quick, light impulse.

To the Teacher: *Continue to demonstrate these warm-ups first. Encourage students to create variations of them by transposing them to different keys.*

Warm-Ups

Soda Pop *pg. 28*

When you pour soda into a glass, the bubbles rise to the surface and pop. They move up effortlessly.

Imitate the fizzy sound of carbonation by playing this piece using little arm weight. Play each two-note slur with one drop/lift motion of the arm and wrist. When you play the grace notes, compress this motion into one impulse, letting the last note rebound naturally.

Stepping Stones *pg. 29*

When you walk a path of stepping stones through a brook or a garden, you step lightly, making a slight pause between each step.

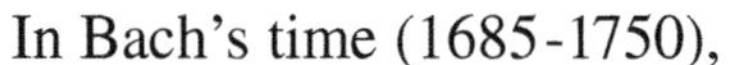

In Bach's time (1685-1750), the most common keyboard instrument was the harpsichord. Unlike the modern piano, the harpsichord is unable to sustain the sound between notes continuously. To imitate the way music sounded on this Baroque instrument, play the quarter notes with a slight break in sound between each one.

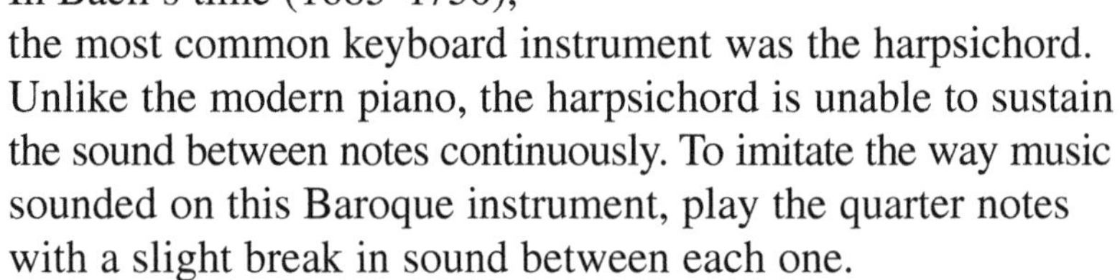

Soda Pop

(♩ = 92)

Stepping Stones

(♩ = 72)

Soda Pop

Effervescently (♩ = 112)

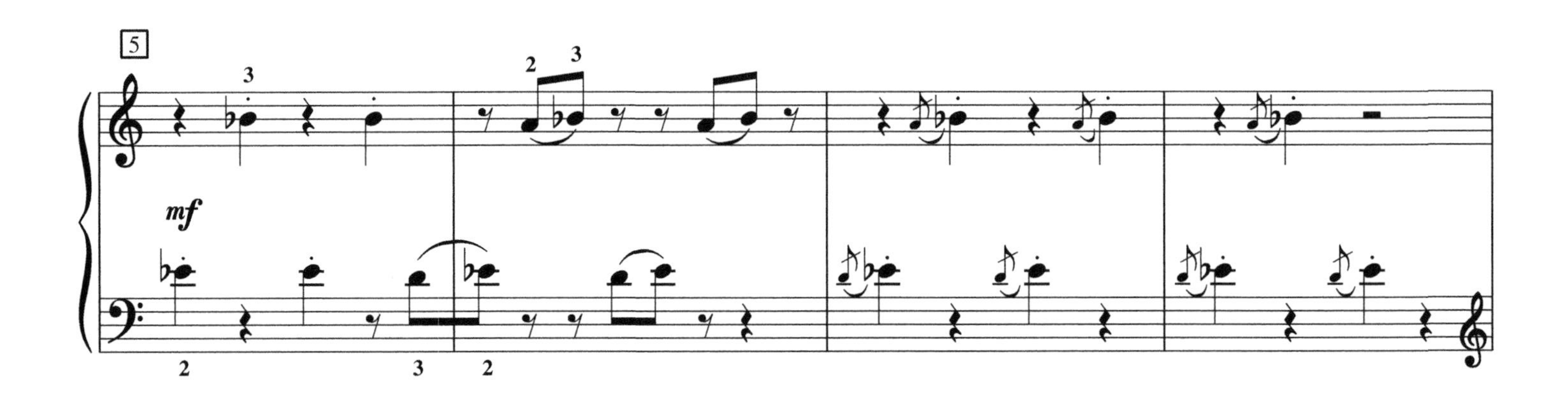

Stepping Stones

Musical Fitness Plan

Use this checklist to review fitness skills and to focus on learning new ones.

☐ **Extending to an Octave**

Playing Blocked Chords in First Inversion
Place your hand in the shape of the first-inversion chord with an interval of a sixth from the bottom note to the top note, and an interval of a third from the bottom note to the middle note.

Playing Blocked Chords in Second Inversion
Place your hand in the shape of the second-inversion chord with an interval of a sixth from the bottom note to the top note, and an interval of a fourth from the bottom note to the middle note.

Keeping the Hand in Position When Playing Parallel Chords
Keep your wrist flexible and your arm relaxed, while retaining the shape of the chord in your hand as you move from place to place on the keyboard.

To the Teacher: *Continue to demonstrate these warm-ups first. Encourage students to create variations of the warm-ups by moving them to different octaves.*

Warm-Ups

Cookie Cutters

A cookie cutter creates the same precise shape each time you press it down. You simply move the cutter from place to place on the dough, being careful to set down all the edges of the cutter at the same time.

Cookie Cutter 1 *pg. 32*

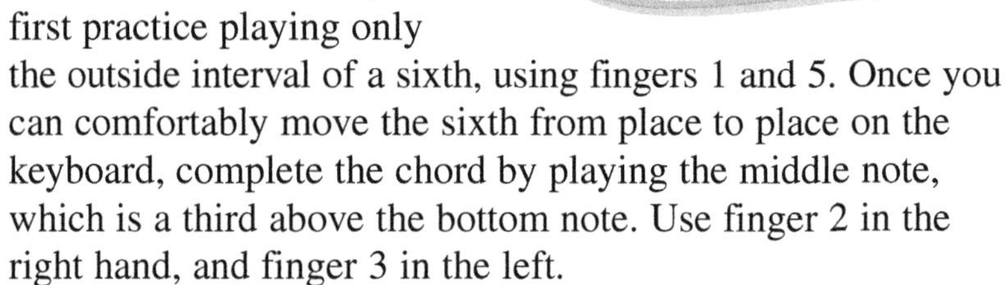

When playing **first-inversion** chords, first practice playing only the outside interval of a sixth, using fingers 1 and 5. Once you can comfortably move the sixth from place to place on the keyboard, complete the chord by playing the middle note, which is a third above the bottom note. Use finger 2 in the right hand, and finger 3 in the left.

Cookie Cutter 2 *pg. 33*

When playing **second-inversion** chords, first practice playing only the outside interval of a sixth, using fingers 1 and 5. Once you can comfortably move the sixth from place to place on the keyboard, complete the chord by playing the middle note, which is a fourth above the bottom note. Use finger 3 in the right hand, and finger 2 in the left.

Play each chord tone with equal arm weight so all three notes sound at exactly the same moment.

When playing broken octaves, keep your hand flexible, letting your wrist take you from note to note as it moves gently from side to side.

Cookie Cutter 1

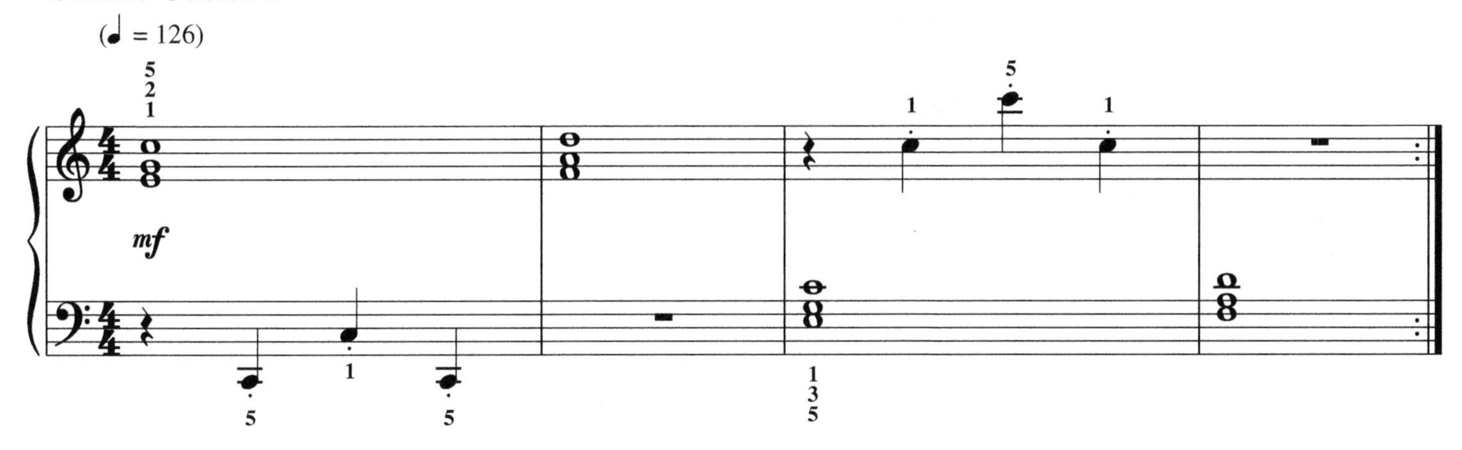

Cookie Cutter 2

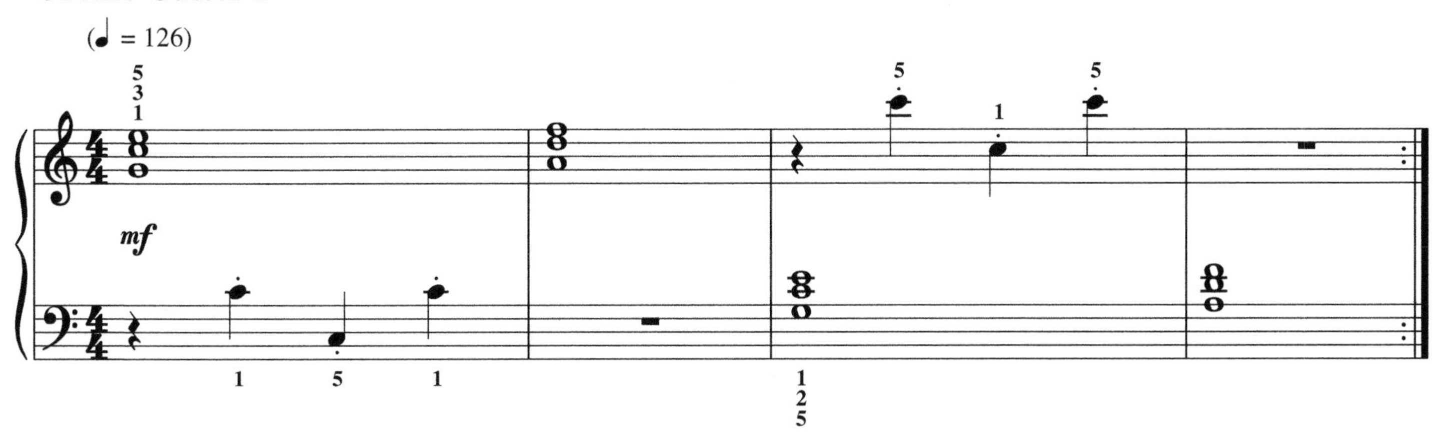

Cookie Cutter 1

Cookie Cutter 2

Use with Lesson Book 5, pg. 31

Musical Fitness Plan

Use this checklist to review fitness skills and to focus on learning new ones.

☐ **Syncopated Pedaling**

☐ **Tucking 1 under 3; Crossing 3 over 1**

Playing a Waltz-Bass Pattern
Practice the bass pattern with your eyes closed, letting your fingers "feel" their way from the single bass note to the two-note interval by lightly touching the black keys as you move.

To the Teacher: Demonstrate these warm-ups first. This will allow students to focus on the purely physical aspects of learning a new skill. Encourage students to play each warm-up in different octaves.

Warm-Ups

Stormy Night *pg. 36*

The wind on a stormy night makes an eerie sound. Sometimes loud, sometimes soft, the howl of the wind announces its strength. Trees bend and sway in the wind's wake, trying to stay rooted in the earth.

Imitate the sound of the wind by shaping the dynamics within each scale passage. Use more arm weight to increase the sound, and less weight to decrease it.

Keep the chords steady, like trees in the wind. When moving from one chord to another, keep the same finger on the common tone. Move to the new notes by changing your hand shape only slightly, making the transition as smooth as possible.

Second Nature *pg. 37*

When you are typing a school report on your computer keyboard, you will do the job better if you don't look at your hands. As your moves become second nature, you will be free to focus your eyes on the manuscript.

The left-hand waltz bass in this etude will become second nature if you play it without looking at your hands. Practice the pattern with your eyes closed, letting your fingers "feel" their way to each new position by lightly touching the black keys as you move.

Once you can play the left-hand accompaniment without looking, you can focus on playing the right-hand melody in one long, arching phrase.

Stormy Night

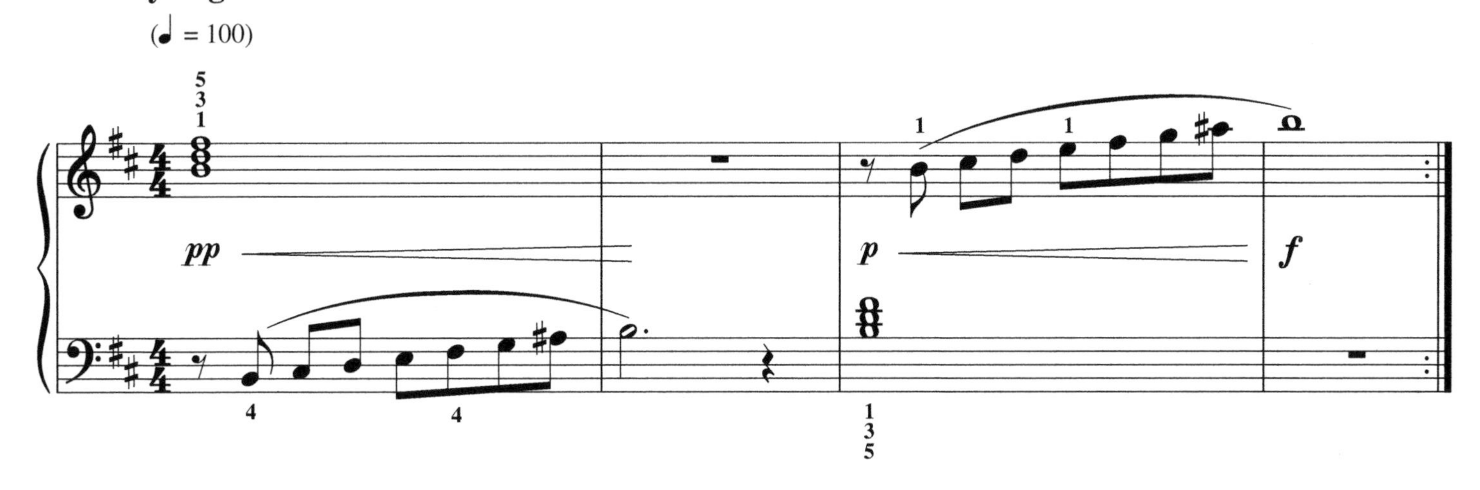

Second Nature

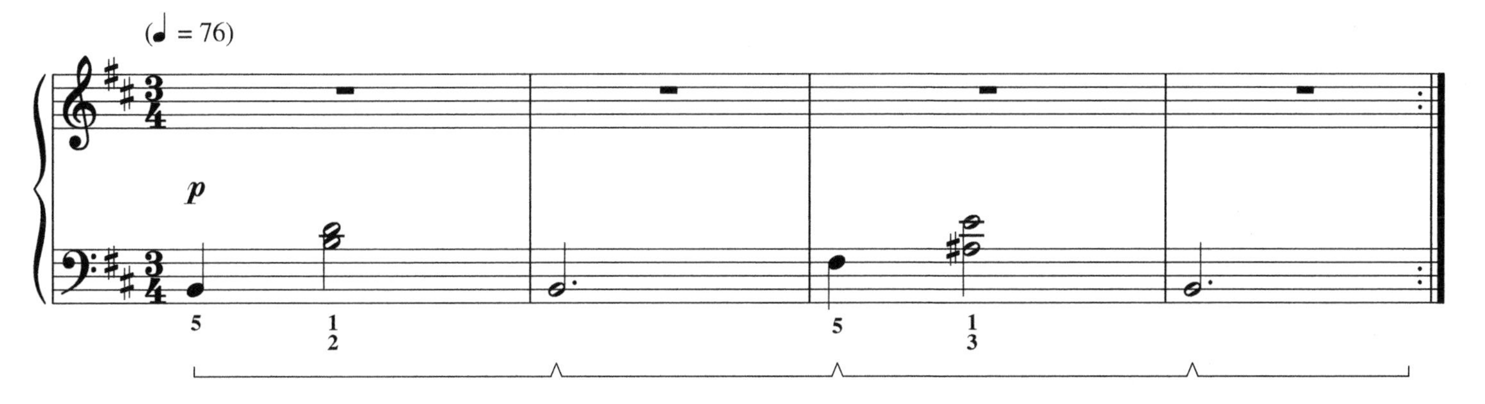

Stormy Night

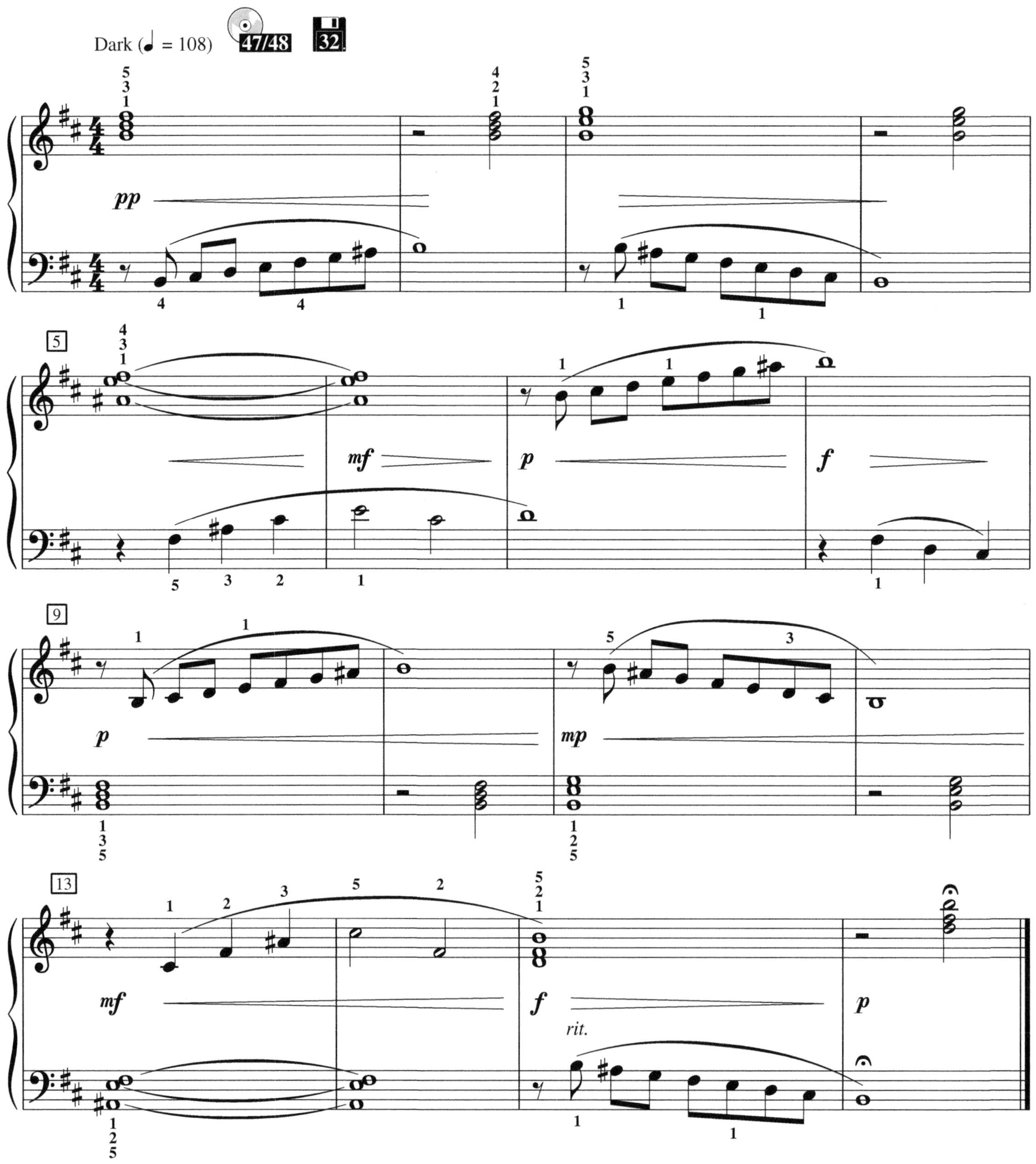

Second Nature

Use with Lesson Book 5, pgs. 34-35

Musical Fitness Plan

Use this checklist to review fitness skills and to focus on learning new ones.

☐ **Accommodating Different Black Keys When Moving from One Scale to Another**

Playing a Chromatic Scale
To play the half steps easily, keep your hand contracted and your fingers close together. Let your arm follow your fingers.

To the Teacher: *Demonstrate these warm-ups first. This will allow students to focus on the purely physical aspects of learning a new skill. Encourage students to play each warm-up in different octaves.*

Warm-Ups

Geometrics *pg. 40*

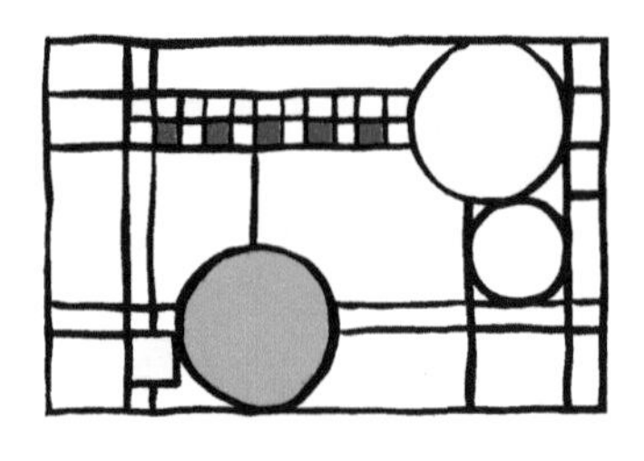

Artists and architects use geometric shapes to create a larger shape or form. Many windows in architect Frank Lloyd Wright's famous prairie-style houses feature primary geometric shapes repeated over and over to make a new artistic design.

Each musical pattern has its own shape and feel. Composers can repeat scales and sequences in various combinations to create a new piece. Use the rests in the etude to prepare your hand for each new pattern.

Play each phrase in one impulse, beginning with a downward motion of your arm and following through with an upward motion of your wrist.

Dominoes *pg. 41*

When you stand a row of dominoes on end and give them a small shove, they fall in order, creating a ripple effect.

Play each phrase in one drop/lift impulse of your arm and wrist. Release the final note in the phrase as soon as you play it. Follow through from hand to hand.

Begin each group of slurred notes softly using little arm weight and get gradually louder by increasing your arm weight to match the dynamics.

Geometrics

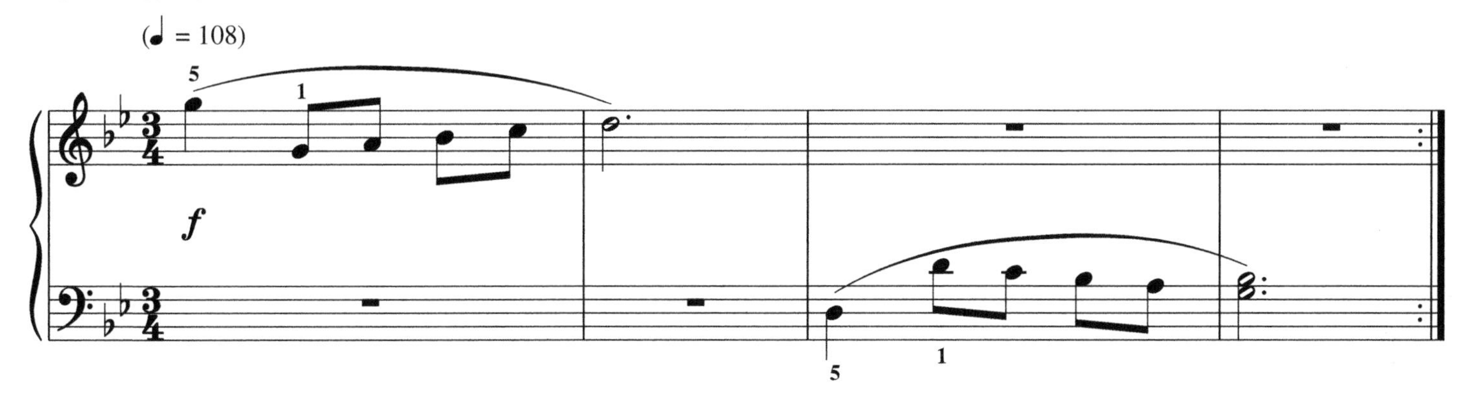

Dominoes

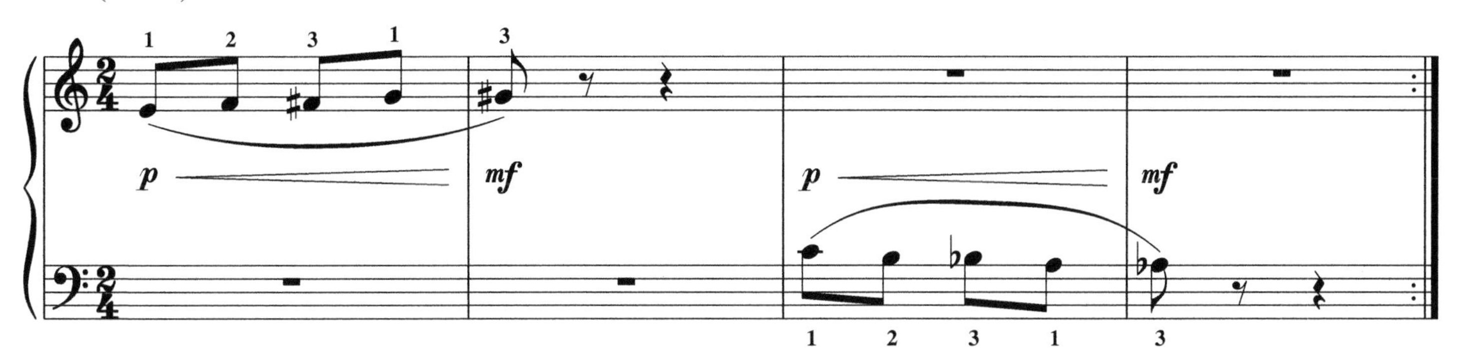

Geometrics

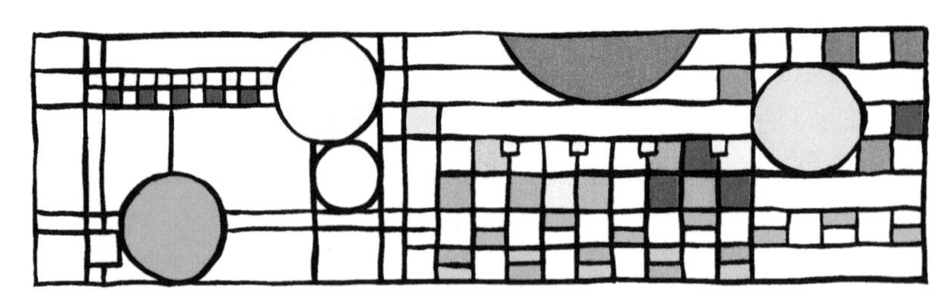

Dominoes

Smoothly (♩ = 90) 55/56 37

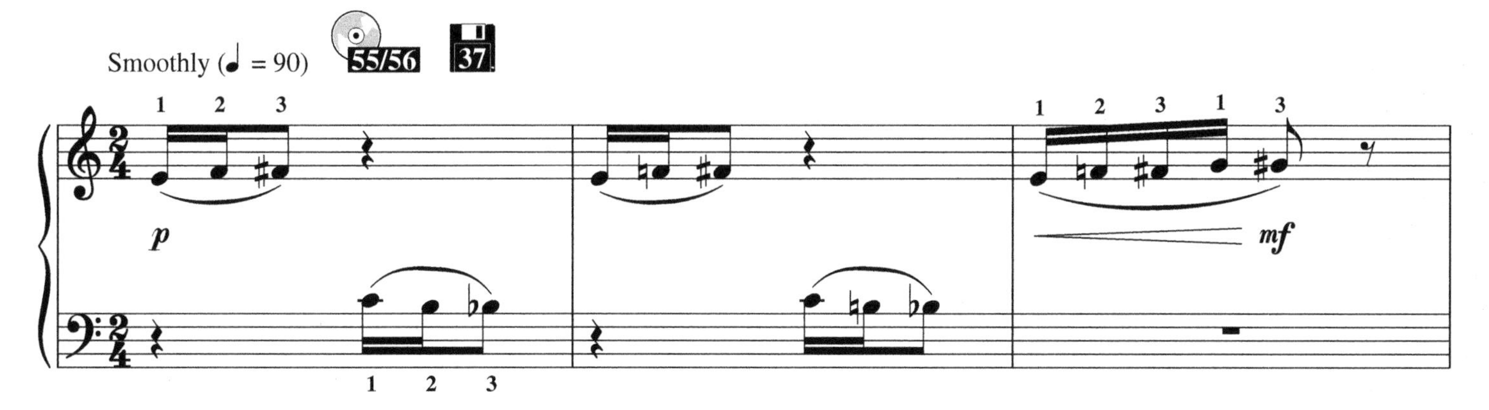

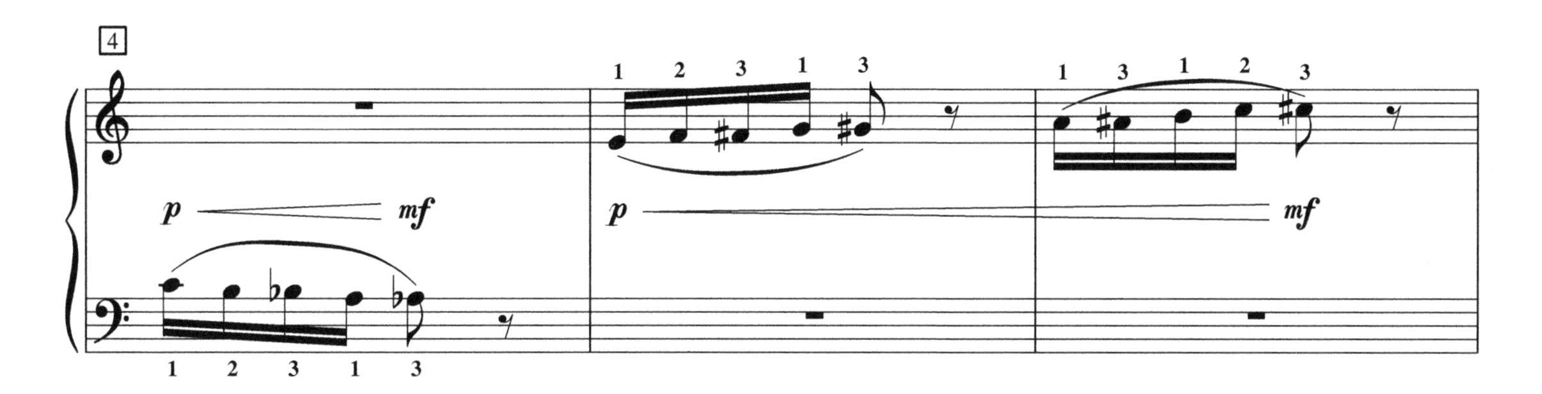

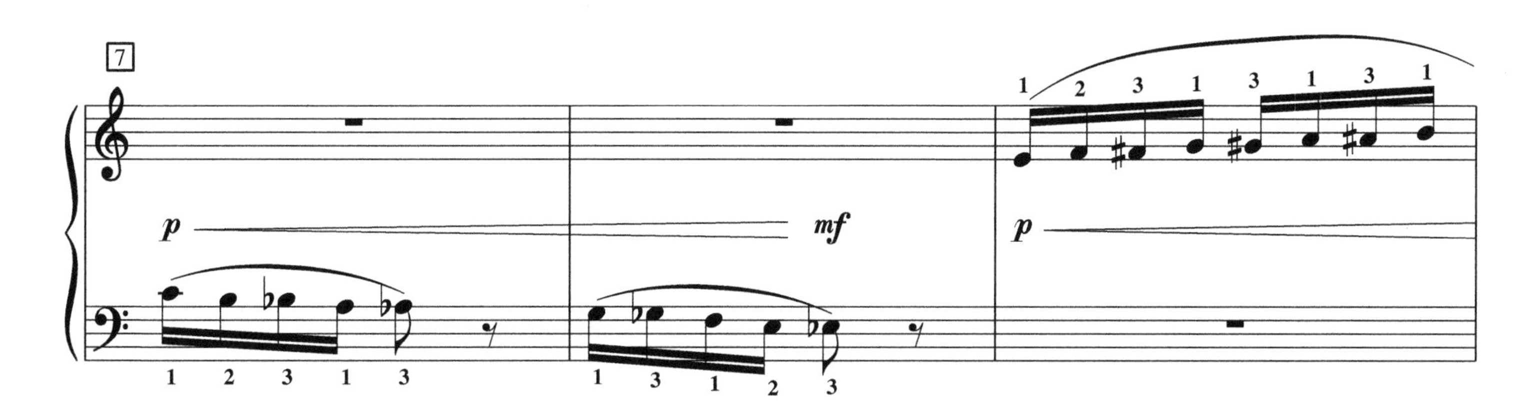

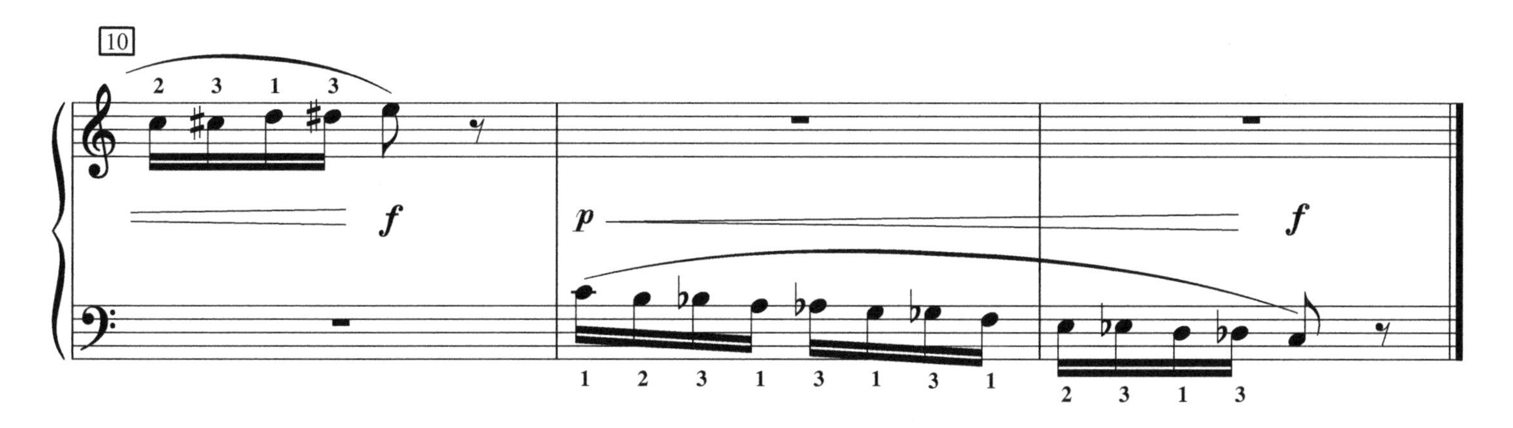

Use with Lesson Book 5, pg. 42

Musical Fitness Plan

Use this checklist to review fitness skills and to focus on learning new ones.

☐ **Extending to an Octave**

☐ **Tucking 1 under 3; Crossing 3 over 1**

☐ **Playing Black-key/White-key Combinations**

☐ **Playing a Chromatic Scale**

Playing Blocked Chords *Legato*
To play blocked chords *legato*, pass the sound smoothly from the top note of one chord to the top note of the next. Play the other chord tones as smoothly as possible, keeping your fingers close to the keys.

To the Teacher: *Continue to demonstrate these warm-ups first. Encourage students to create variations of the warm-ups by moving them to different octaves.*

Warm-Ups

Blind Alley *pg. 44*

When you ride your bike through an alley, you never know what is around the corner. Some alleys are wide and some are narrow. You need to vary the way you navigate each one, taking time to stop and check before you ride out into the traffic.

When varying your hand shape from the extended one necessary to play broken chords to the contracted one appropriate for chromatic passages, keep your hand and wrist flexible. Use the rests to gauge the distance between fingers you will need for the next phrase.

Even Keel *pg. 45*

When navigating a boat over a choppy sea, the captain tries to keep an even keel so the boat will remain upright and move along as smoothly as possible.

When playing a phrase that requires the thumb to move from white key to black key to white, you can keep an even keel – a smooth sound – by moving your fingers slightly forward into the black keys to accommodate the different heights between keys.

For a more *legato* sound, change the usual 1-3-5 chord fingering to 1-2-4. Although you will still hear a slight break in sound between tones in the right hand, the smooth movement will create the illusion of *legato*.

Blind Alley

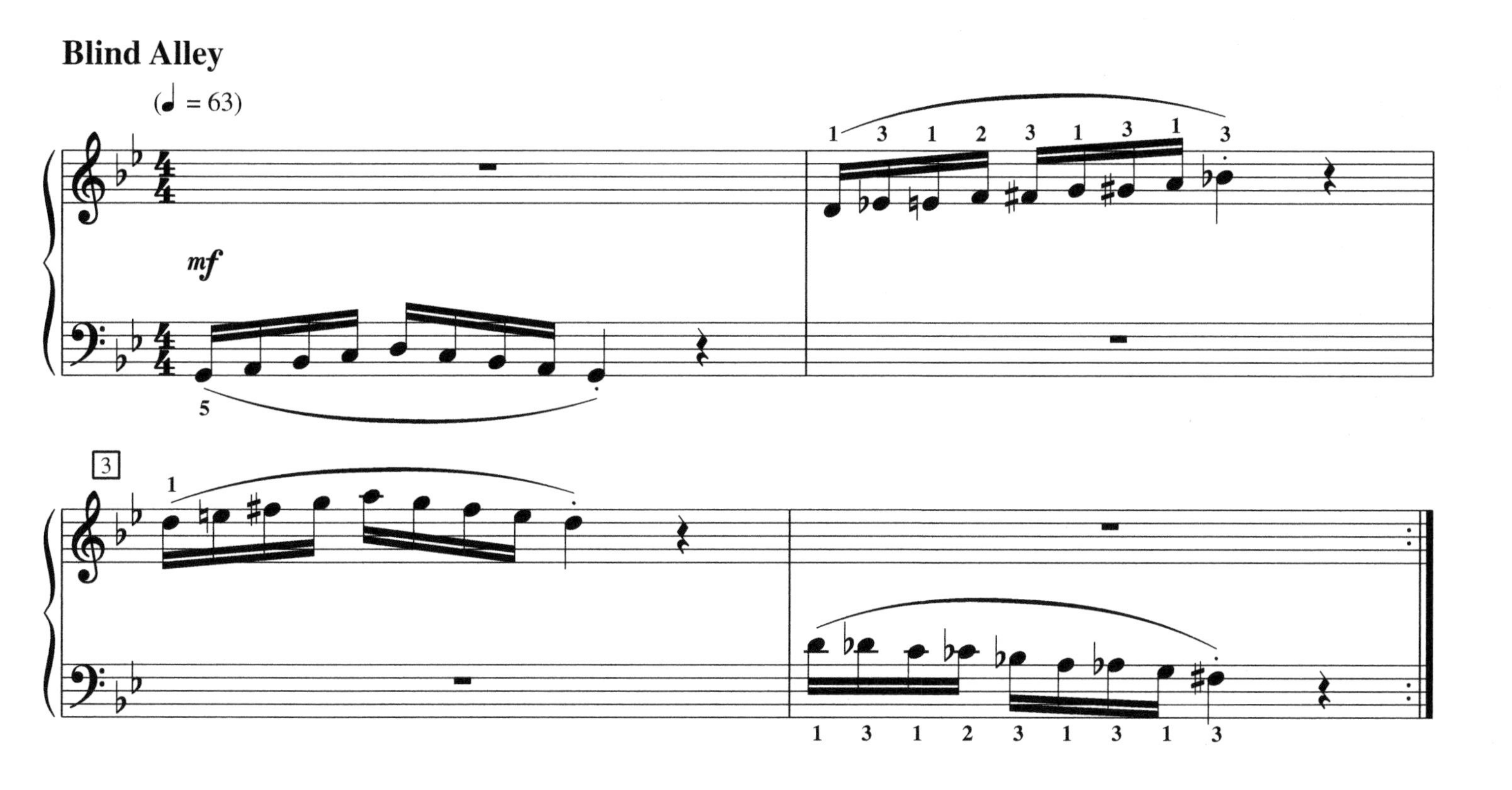

Even Keel

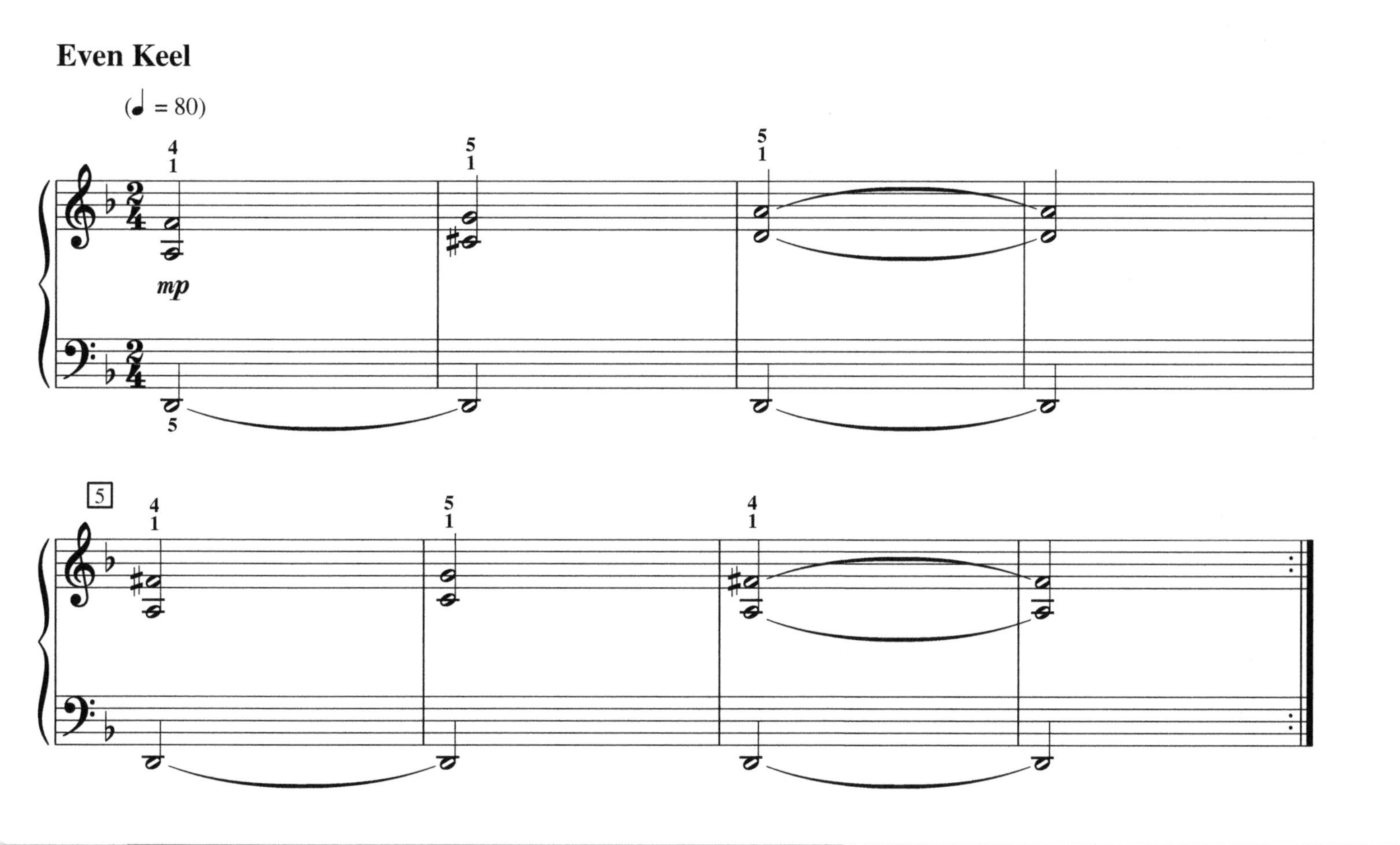

Blind Alley

Even Keel

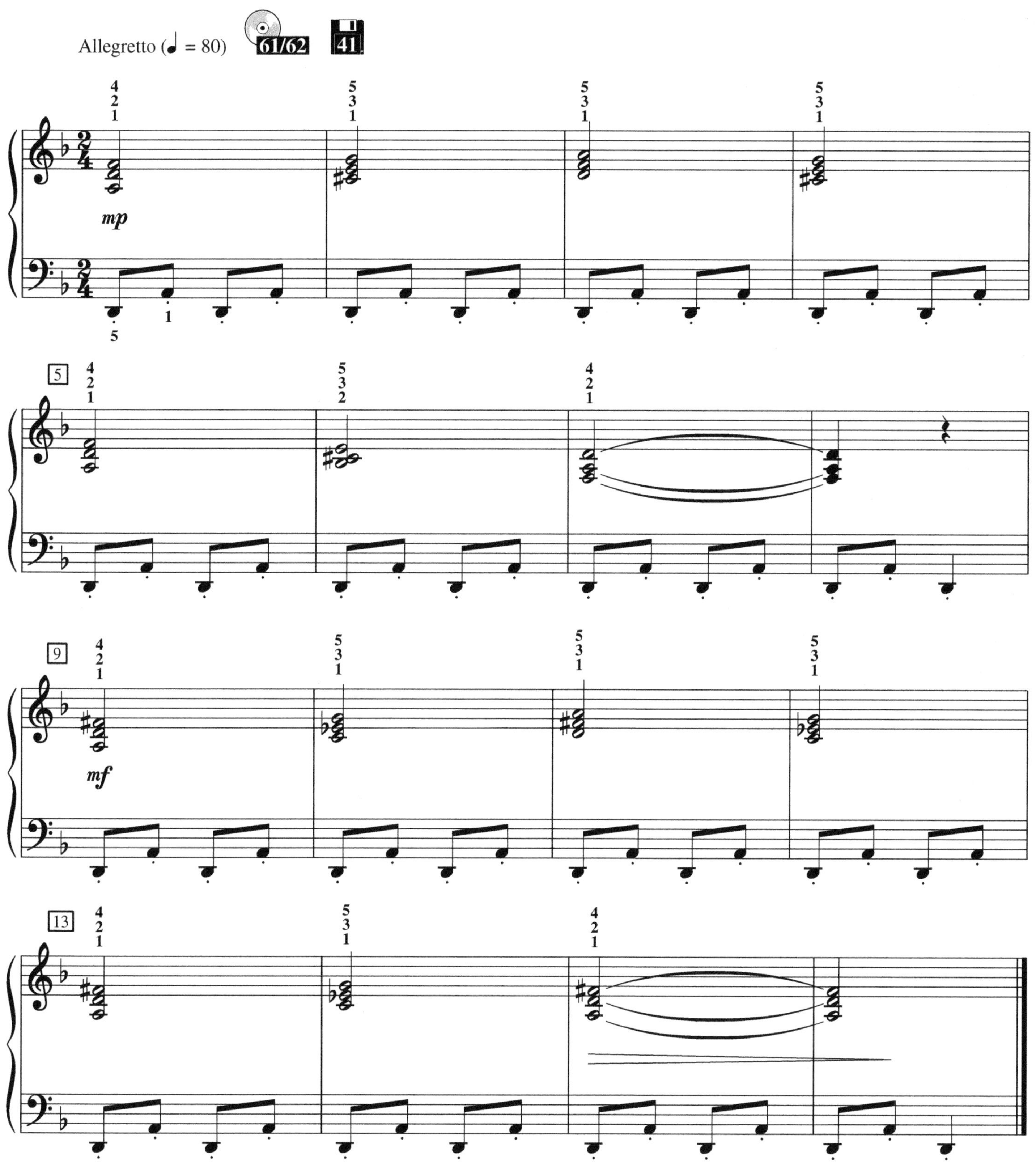

Use with Lesson Book 5, pgs. 44-45

Musical Fitness Plan

Combining Patterns of First and Second Inversion Chords
When moving from one chord to the next, move your hand as little as possible. Keep the same finger on the common tone between chords.

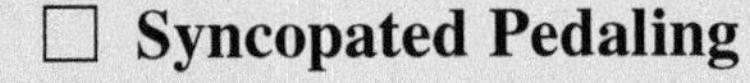

☐ **Syncopated Pedaling**

Warm-Up

Ceremony *pg. 47*  

At important ceremonies, such as graduations or weddings, participants move from place to place in procession. If you have ever seen the ring bearer and the flower girl in a wedding, remember how they moved at a slow pace down the aisle, taking careful, exactly measured steps.

When moving from one chord to the next, move your hand as little as possible. Choose the closest way for each finger to get from one chord tone to the next. Pass the sound from finger to finger, creating the smoothest possible sound.

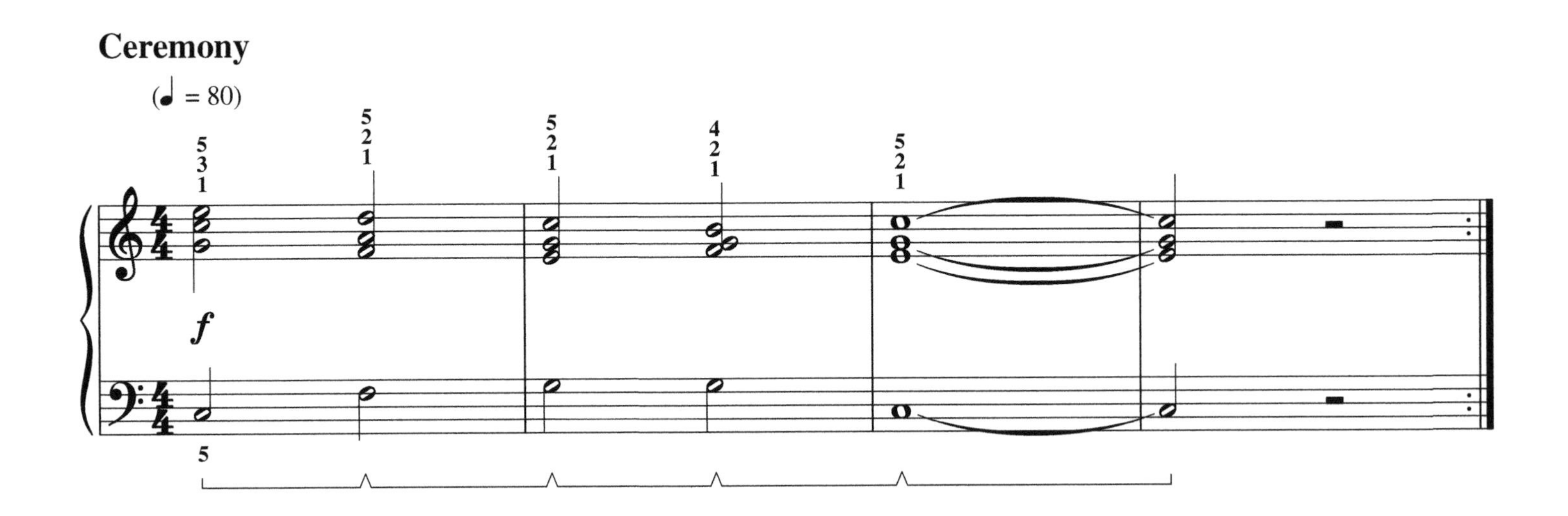

Ceremony

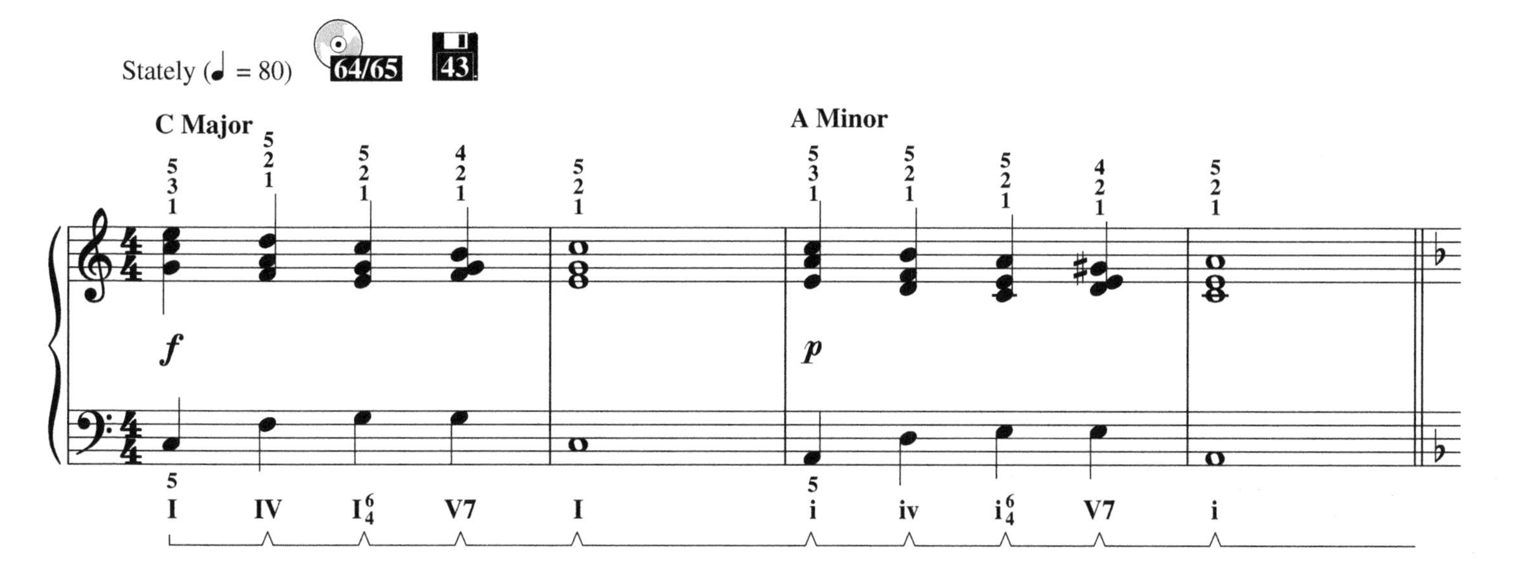

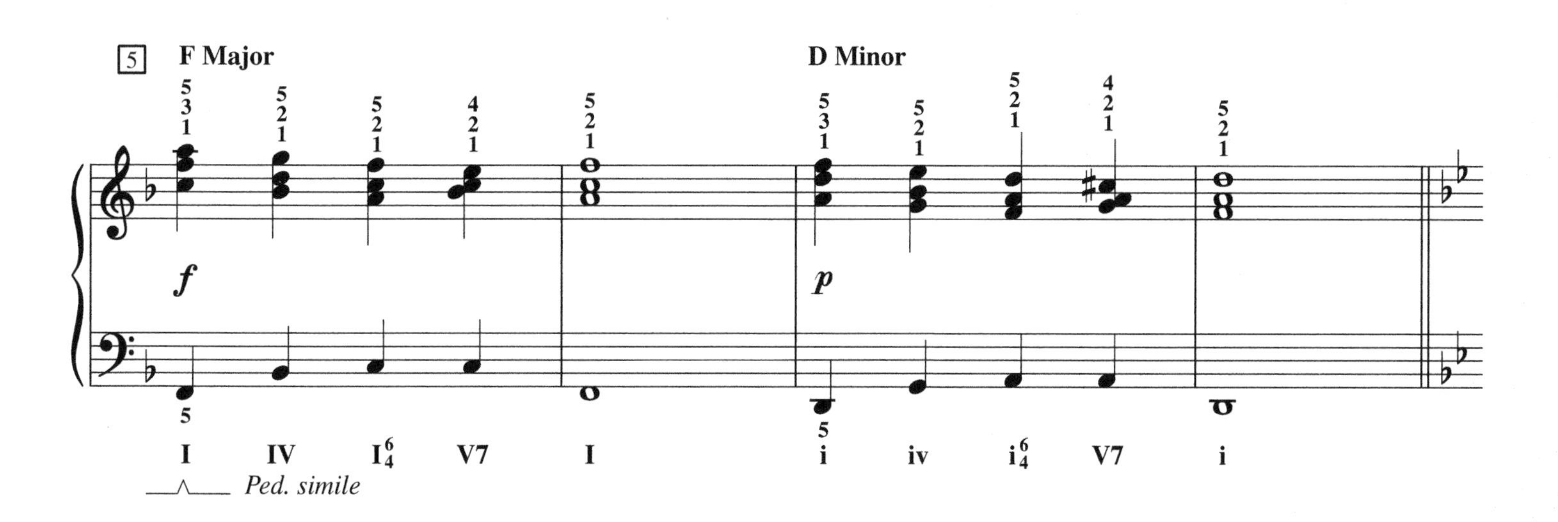

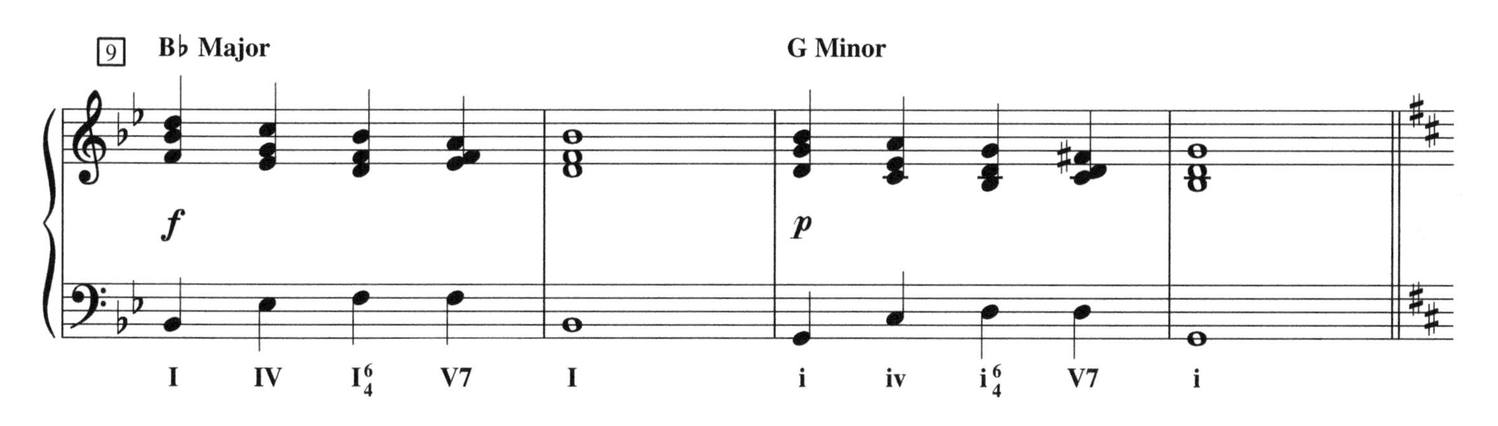

Use with Lesson Book 5, pgs. 47-50

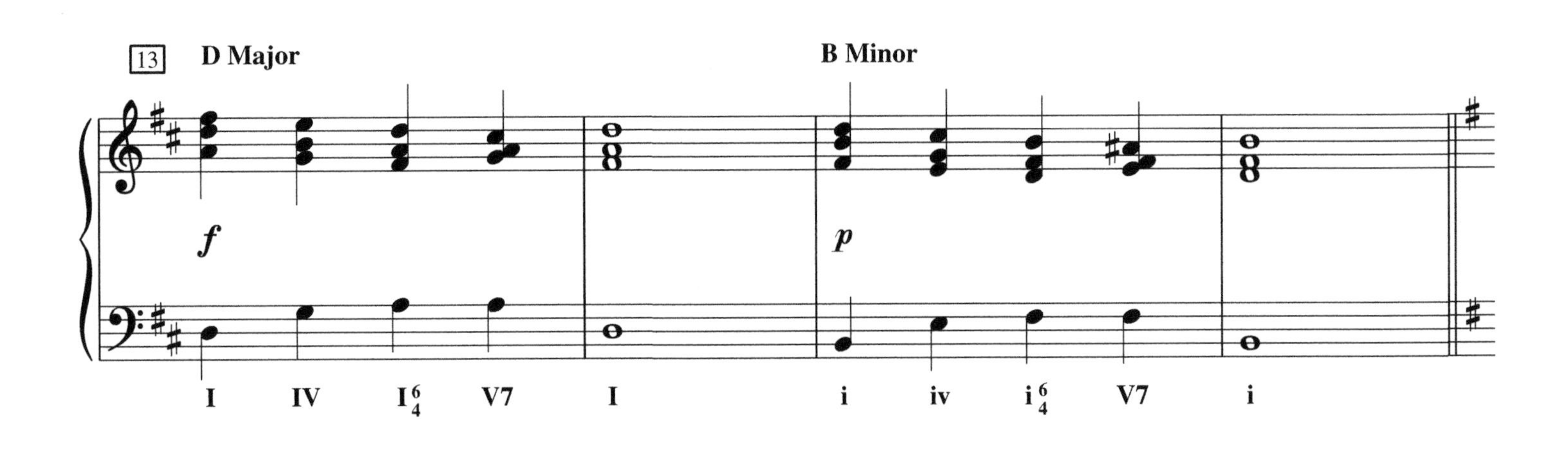
13
D Major
B Minor
f
p
I
IV
I 6 4
V7
I
i
iv
i 6 4
V7
i

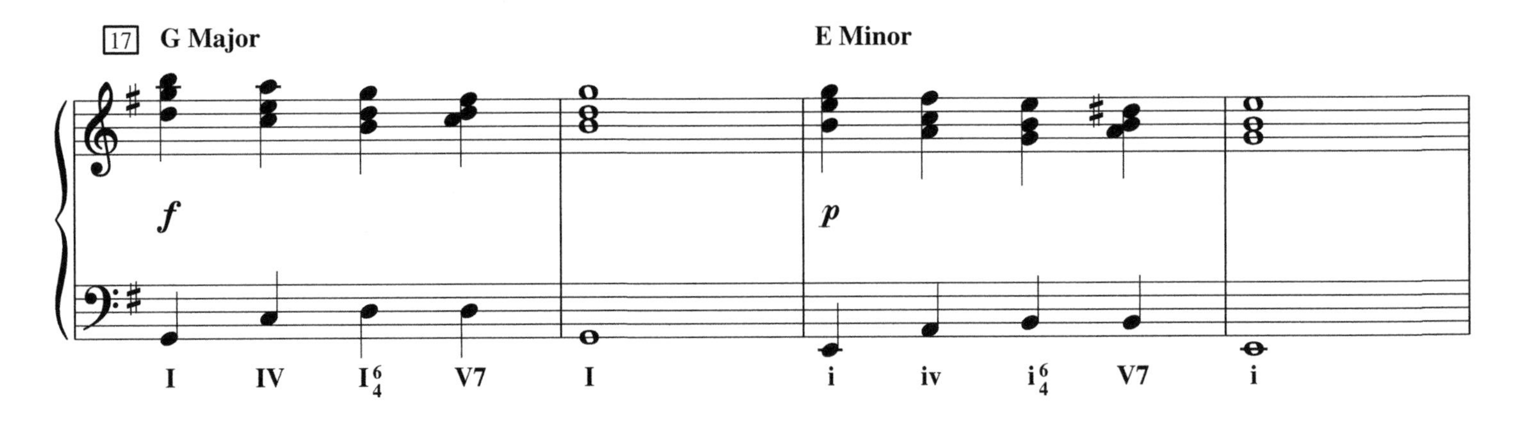
17
G Major
E Minor
f
p
I
IV
I 6 4
V7
I
i
iv
i 6 4
V7
i

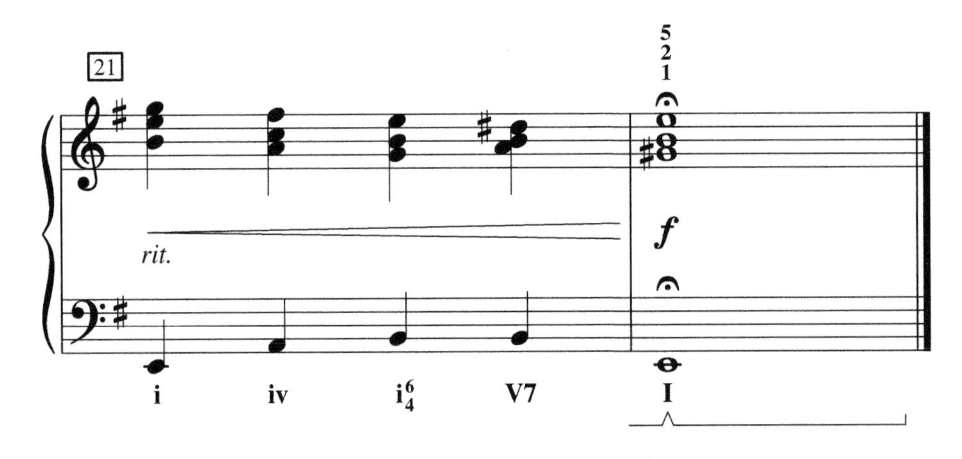
21
5
2
1
rit.
f
i
iv
i 6 4
V7
I